# Life in the UK Test Handbook 2022 Edition

*Everything you need to PASS the Life in the UK test first time around*

Edited by L. M. Sweeney LL.B

ISBN: 9798831455533 (Paperback)

**Chapter 1 - The Values and Principles of the UK**    **7**

    Becoming a permanent resident    8

    Taking the Life in the UK Test    8

**Chapter 2 - What is the UK?**    **10**

**Chapter 3 - A Long and Illustrious History**    **12**

    Early Britain    12

    The Romans    13

    The Anglo-Saxons    13

    The Vikings    14

    The Norman Conquest    14

    The Middle Ages    15

    War at home and abroad    15

    The Black Death    16

    Legal and political changes    17

    A Distinct Identity    17

    The Wars of The Roses    18

    The Tudors and Stuarts    19

    Queen Elizabeth I    21

    The Reformation in Scotland and Mary, Queen of Scots    21

    Exploration, poetry and drama    22

    James VI and I    22

    The King James Bible    22

    Ireland    23

    The Rise of Parliament    23

    The beginning of the English Civil War    24

    Oliver Cromwell & The English Republic    24

    The Restoration    25

    Isaac Newton (1643-1727)    26

    A Catholic king    26

    The Glorious Revolution    26

    Constitutional monarchy – the Bill of Rights    27

    A Growing Population    28

    The Act or Treaty of Union in Scotland    29

    The Prime Minister    29

    The rebellion of the clans    30

    Robert Burns (1759-96)    30

    The Enlightenment    31

    The Industrial Revolution    31

    Richard Arkwright (1732-92)    32

    Sake Dean Mahomet (1759-1851)    32

The slave trade                                              33
The American War of Independence                             33
War with France                                             34
The Union Flag                                              34
The Victorian Age                                           35
Trade and industry                                          35
Isambard Kingdom Brunel (1806-59)                           36
The Crimean War                                             36
Florence Nightingale (1820-1910)                            36
The right to vote                                           37
Emmeline Pankhurst (1858-1928)                              38
The future of the Empire                                    38
Rudyard Kipling (1865-1936)                                 39
The First World War                                         40
The partition of Ireland                                    41
The inter-war period                                        42
The Second World War                                        43
Winston Churchill (1874-1965)                               44
Alexander Fleming (1881-1955)                               45
The Welfare State                                           45
Clement Attlee (1883-1967)                                  46
William Beveridge (1879-1963)                               46
R A Butler (1902-82)                                        46
Dylan Thomas (1914-53)                                      47
Migration in Post-war Britain                               47
Social change in the 1960s                                  48
Problem in the economy in the 1970s                         50
Mary Peters (1939-)                                         50
Europe and the Common Market                                50
Conservative government from 1979 to 1997                   50
Margaret Thatcher (1925-2013)                               51
Roald Dahl (1916-90)                                        51
Labour government from 1997 to 2010                         52
Conflicts in Afghanistan and Iraq                           52
Coalition government 2010 onwards                           52

**Chapter 4 - A Modern, Thriving Society**                  **54**
The UK today                                                54
Languages and dialects                                      54
Population                                                  54
Ethnic diversity                                            55

An Equal Society                                         55
Religion                                                56
Christian churches                                      56
Patron saints' days                                    57
Customs and traditions                                 58
Other religious festivals                              58
Other festivals and traditions                         59
Bank Holidays                                          59
Sport                                                  60
Notable British sportsmen and women                    60
Cricket                                                62
Football                                               62
Rugby                                                  63
Horse Racing                                           63
Golf                                                   63
Tennis                                                 63
Water Sports                                           63
Motor sports                                           64
Skiing                                                 64
Arts and culture                                       64
Theatre                                                66
Art                                                    67
Notable British artists                                67
Architecture                                           68
Fashion and design                                     69
Literature                                             69
Notable authors and writers                            70
British Poets                                           71
Leisure                                                72
Gardening                                              72
Shopping                                               72
Cooking and food                                       73
Traditional foods                                      73
British film industry                                  73
British comedy                                         74
Television and radio                                   75
Social networking                                      76
Pubs and night clubs                                   76
Betting and gambling                                   76
Pets                                                   76
Places of interest                                     77

UK Landmarks                                                          77

**Chapter 5 - The UK Government, the Law and Your Role          80**
The development of British democracy                                  80
The British constitution                                             81
Constitutional institutions                                         81
The monarchy                                                        81
The National Anthem                                                 82
System of Government                                                82
The House of Commons                                               83
The House of Lords                                                 83
Elections                                                          84
The Prime Minister                                                 85
The cabinet                                                        85
The opposition                                                     86
The party system                                                   86
The civil service                                                  86
Local government                                                   86
Devolved administrations                                           87
The Welsh government                                               87
The Scottish Parliament                                            87
The Northern Ireland Assembly                                      88
The media and government                                           89
Who can vote?                                                      89
The electoral register                                             90
Where to vote                                                       90
Standing for office                                                91
The UK Parliament                                                  91
The UK and international institutions                              92
The European Union                                                 93
The Council of Europe                                              93
The United Nations                                                 93
The North Atlantic Treaty Organization (NATO)                     94
Respecting the law                                                94
The law in the UK                                                 94
Terrorism and extremism                                           96
The judiciary                                                     97
Criminal courts                                                   97
Magistrates' and Justice of the Peace Courts                      97
Crown Courts and Sheriff Courts                                   97
Youth Courts                                                      98

Civil Courts                                          99
The small claims procedure                            99
Legal Advice                                          99
Fundamental principles                               100
Domestic violence                                    101
Female genital mutilation                            101
Forced marriage                                      101
Income Tax                                           101
National Insurance                                   102
Getting a National Insurance number                  102
Driving                                              102
Your role in the community                           103
Being a good neighbour                               104
Getting involved in local activities                 104
Helping in schools                                   104
School governors and school boards                   104
Supporting political parties                         105
Helping with local services                          105
Blood and organ donation                             105
Other ways to volunteer                              106
Looking after the environment                        107

**Practice Tests**                                   **108**
Practice Test 1                                      108
Practice Test 2                                      111
Practice Test 3                                      114
Answers to Practice Test 1                           117
Answers to Practice Test 2                           121
Answers to Practice Test 3                           124
Revision Crosswords                                  128
Famous Faces                                         132

# Chapter 1 - The Values and Principles of the UK

All British citizens must respect the individual liberties, values and principles the UK was established upon. These values have evolved over 1000 years of British history, tradition and customs and are a fundamental part of what it means to be British.

The fundamental principles of British life include:

- Democracy
- The rule of law
- Individual liberty
- Tolerance of those with different faiths and beliefs
- Participation in community life

You will attend a citizenship ceremony where you will be granted citizenship by a local official, as a new citizen you will take a pledge to uphold the values above.

The official pledge is: 'I will give my loyalty to the United Kingdom and respect its rights and freedoms. I will uphold its democratic values. I will observe its laws faithfully and fulfil my duties and obligations as a British citizen.'

If you wish to be a permanent resident or citizen of the UK, you should:

• Obey the law and the spirit of the law
• Be respectful of the rights of other people, including their freedom of expression
• Look after and provide for you and your family
• Look after those in your community and the area you live in

As a British citizen you will have the RIGHT to:

• Freedom of belief and religion
• Freedom of speech
• Freedom from illegal discrimination
• A right to a fair trial
• A right to join in the elections

# Becoming a permanent resident

To apply to become a permanent resident or citizen of the UK, you will need to:

• Speak and read English
• Have a good understanding of life in the UK.

There are currently (as of January 2013) two ways you can be tested on these requirements:

• Pass the Life in the UK test

AND

• Produce acceptable evidence of speaking and listening skills in English at B1 of the Common European Framework of Reference. This is equivalent to ESOL Entry Level 3. The requirements for citizenship applications may also change in the future.

Further details will be published on the UK Border Agency website and you should check the information on that website for current requirements before applying for settlement or citizenship.

# Taking the Life in the UK Test

This handbook will help prepare you for taking the Life in the UK test. The test consists of 24 questions about important aspects of life in the UK. Questions are based on ALL parts of the handbook. The 24 questions will be different for each person taking the test at that test session. The Life in the UK test is usually taken in English, although special arrangements can be made if you wish to take it in Welsh or Scottish Gaelic.

You can only take the test at a registered and approved Life in the UK test centre. There are about 60 test centres around the UK.

You can only book your test online, at www.lifeintheuktest.gov.uk. You should not take your test at any other establishment as the UK Border Agency will only accept certificates from registered test centres.

 If you live on the Isle of Man or in the Channel Islands, there are different arrangements for taking the Life in the UK test. When booking your test, read the instructions carefully. Make sure you enter your details correctly.

You will need to take some identification and proof of your address with you to the test. If you don't take these, you will not be able to take your test. How to use this handbook Everything that you will need to know to pass the Life in the UK test is included in this handbook. The questions will be based on the whole book, including this introduction, so make sure you study the entire book thoroughly.

The handbook has been written to ensure that anyone who can read English at ESOL Entry Level 3 or above should have no difficulty with the language. The glossary at the back of the handbook contains some key words and phrases, which you might find helpful. The 'Check that you understand' boxes are for guidance. They will help you to identify particular things that you should understand. Just knowing the things highlighted in these boxes will not be enough to pass the test.

You need to make sure that you understand everything in the book, so please read the information carefully. Where to find more information You can find out more information from the following places:

• The UK Border Agency website (www.ukba.homeoffice.gov.uk) for more information about the application process and the forms you will need to complete

• The Life in the UK test website (www.lifeintheuktest.gov.uk) for more information about the test and how to book a place to take one

• Gov.uk (www.gov.uk) for information about ESOL courses and how to find one in your area.

**Check that you understand**

• **The origin of the values underlying British society**
• **The fundamental principles of British life**
• **The responsibilities and freedoms which come with permanent residence**
• **The process of becoming a permanent resident or citizen**

# Chapter 2 - What is the UK?

The UK is made up of England, Scotland, Wales and Northern Ireland. The rest of Ireland is an independent country. The official name of the country is the United Kingdom of Great Britain and Northern Ireland. 'Great Britain' refers only to England, Scotland and Wales, not to Northern Ireland. The words 'Britain', 'British Isles' or 'British', however, are used in this book to refer to everyone in the UK. There are also several islands which are closely linked with the UK but are not part of it: the Channel Islands and the Isle of Man.

These have their own governments and are called 'Crown dependencies'. There are also several British overseas territories in other parts of the world, such as St Helena and the Falkland Islands. They are also linked to the UK but are not part of it. The UK is governed by the parliament sitting in Westminster. Scotland, Wales and Northern Ireland also have parliaments or assemblies of their own, with devolved powers in defined areas.

# Chapter 3 - A Long and Illustrious History

## Early Britain

The first people to live in Britain were hunter-gatherers, in what we call the Stone Age. For much of the Stone Age, Britain was connected to the continent by a land bridge. People came and went, following the herds of deer and horses which they hunted. Britain only became permanently separated from the continent by the Channel about 10,000 years ago. The first farmers arrived in Britain 6,000 years ago. The ancestors of these first farmers probably came from south-east Europe. These people built houses, tombs and monuments on the land. One of these monuments, Stonehenge, still stands in what is now the English county of Wiltshire. Stonehenge was probably a special gathering place for seasonal ceremonies. Other Stone Age sites have also survived. Skara Brae on Orkney, off the north coast of Scotland, is the best preserved prehistoric village in northern Europe, and has helped archaeologists to understand more about how people lived near the end of the Stone Age.

Around 4,000 years ago, people learned to make bronze. We call this period the Bronze Age. People lived in roundhouses and buried their dead in tombs called round barrows. The people of the Bronze Age were accomplished metalworkers who made many beautiful objects in bronze and gold, including tools, ornaments and weapons. The Bronze Age was followed by the Iron Age, when people learned how to make weapons and tools out of iron. People still lived in roundhouses grouped together into larger settlements, and sometimes defended sites called hill forts. A very impressive hill fort can still be seen today at Maiden Castle, in the English county of Dorset. Most people were farmers, craft workers or warriors. The language they spoke was part of the Celtic language family. Similar languages were spoken across Europe in the Iron Age and related languages are still spoken today in some parts of Wales, Scotland and Ireland. The people of the Iron Age had a sophisticated culture and economy. They made the first coins to be minted in Britain, some inscribed with the names of Iron Age kings. This marks the beginnings of British history.

# The Romans

Julius Caesar led a Roman invasion of Britain in 55 BC. This was unsuccessful and for nearly 100 years Britain remained separate from the Roman Empire. In AD 43 the Emperor Claudius led the Roman army in a new invasion. This time, there was resistance from some of the British tribes but the Romans were successful in occupying almost all of Britain. One of the tribal leaders who fought against the Romans was Boudicca, the queen of the Iceni in what is now eastern England. She is still remembered today and there is a statue of her on Westminster Bridge in London, near the Houses of Parliament. Areas of what is now Scotland were never conquered by the Romans, and the Emperor Hadrien built a wall in the north of England to keep out the Picts (ancestors of the Scottish people). Included in the wall were a number of forts. Parts of Hadrien's Wall, including the forts of Housesteads and Vindolanda, can still be seen. It is a popular area for walkers and is a UNESCO (United Nations Educational Scientific and Cultural Organization) World Heritage Site. The Romans remained in Britain for 400 years. They built roads and public buildings, created a structure of law, and introduced new plants and animals. It was during the 3rd and 4th centuries AD that the first Christian communities began to appear in Britain.

# The Anglo-Saxons

The Roman army left Britain in AD 410 to defend other parts of the Roman Empire and never returned. Britain was again invaded by tribes from northern Europe: the Jutes, the Angles and the Saxons. The languages they spoke are the basis of modern-day English. Battles were fought against these invaders but, by about AD 600, Anglo-Saxon kingdoms were established in Britain. These kingdoms were mainly in what is now England. The burial place of one of the kings was at Sutton Hoo in modern Suffolk. This king was buried with treasure and armour, all placed in a ship which was then covered by a mound of earth. Parts of the west of Britain, including much of what is now Wales, and Scotland, remained free of Anglo-Saxon rule. The Anglo-Saxons were not Christians when they first came to Britain but, during this period, missionaries came to Britain to preach about Christianity. Missionaries from Ireland spread the religion in the north. The most famous of these were St Patrick, who would become the patron saint of Ireland, and St Columba, who founded a monastery on the island of Iona, off the coast of what is now Scotland. St Augustine led missionaries from Rome, who spread Christianity in the south. St Augustine became the first Archbishop of Canterbury.

## The Vikings

The Vikings came from Denmark and Norway. They first visited Britain in AD 789 to raid coastal towns and take away goods and slaves. Then, they began to stay and form their own communities in the east of England and Scotland. The Anglo-Saxon kingdoms in England united under King Alfred the Great, who defeated the Vikings. Many of the Viking invaders stayed in Britain – especially in the east and north of England in an area known as the Danelaw (many place names there, such as Grimsby and Scunthorpe come from the Viking languages). The Viking settlers mixed with local communities and some converted to Christianity. Anglo-Saxon kings continued to rule what is now England, except for a short period when there were Danish kings. The first of these was Cnut, also named Canute. In the north, the threat of attack by Vikings had encouraged the people to unite under one king, Kenneth MacAlpin. The term Scotland began to be used to describe that country.

## The Norman Conquest

In 1066, an invasion led by William, the Duke of Normandy (in what is now northern France), defeated Harold, the Saxon king of England, at the Battle of Hastings. Harold was killed in the battle. William became king of England and is known as William the Conqueror. The battle is commemorated in a great piece of embroidery, known as the Bayeux tapestry, which can still be seen in France today.

The Norman Conquest was the last successful foreign invasion of England and led to many changes in government and social structures in England. Norman French, the language of the new ruling class influenced the development of the English language as we know it today. Initially the Normans also conquered Wales, but the Welsh gradually won territory back. The Scots and the Normans fought on the border between England and Scotland; the Normans took over some land on the border but did not invade Scotland. William sent people all over England to draw up lists of all the towns and villages. The people who lived there, who owned the land and what animals they owned were also listed. This was called the

Domesday Book. It still exists today and gives a picture of society in England just after the Norman Conquest.

**Check that you understand**

• **The history of the UK before the Romans**
• **The impact of the Romans on British society**
• **The different groups that invaded after the Romans**
• **The importance of the Norman invasion in 1066**

# The Middle Ages

# War at home and abroad

The period after the Norman Conquest up until about 1485 is called the Middle Ages (or the medieval period). It was a time of almost constant war. The English kings fought with the Welsh, Scottish and Irish noblemen for control of their lands. In Wales, the English were able to establish their rule. In 1284 King Edward I of England introduced the Statute of Rhuddlan, which annexed Wales to the Crown of England. Huge castles, including Conwy and Caenarvon, were built to maintain this power. By the middle of the 15th century the last Welsh rebellions had been defeated. English laws and the English language were introduced. In Scotland, the English kings were less successful. In 1314 the Scottish, led by Robert the Bruce, defeated the English at the Battle of Bannockburn, and Scotland remained unconquered by the English.

At the beginning of the Middle Ages, Ireland was an independent country. The English first went to Ireland as troops to help the Irish king and remained to build their own settlements. By 1200, the English ruled an area of Ireland known as the Pale, around Dublin. Some of the important lords in other parts of Ireland accepted the authority of the English king. During the Middle Ages, the English kings also fought a number of wars abroad. Many knights took part in the Crusades, in which European Christians fought for control of the Holy Land. English kings also fought a long war with France, called the Hundred Years War (even though it actually lasted 116 years). One of the most famous battles of the Hundred Years War was the Battle of Agincourt in 1415, where King Henry V's vastly outnumbered English army defeated the French. The English left France in the 1450s.

## The Black Death

The Normans used a system of land ownership known as feudalism. The king gave land to his lords in return for help in war. Landowners had to send certain numbers of men to serve in the army. Some peasants had their own land but most were serfs. They had a small area of their lord's land where they could grow food. In return, they had to work for their lord and could not move away. The same system developed in southern Scotland. In the north of Scotland and Ireland, land was owned by members of the 'clans' (prominent families). In 1348, a disease, probably a form of plague, came to Britain. This was known as the Black Death. One third of the population of England died and a similar proportion in Scotland and Wales. This was one of the worst disasters ever to strike Britain. Following the Black Death, the smaller population meant there was less need to grow cereal crops. There were labour shortages and peasants began to demand higher wages. New social classes appeared, including owners of large areas of land (later called the gentry), and people left the countryside to live in the towns. In the towns, growing wealth led to the development of a strong middle class. In Ireland, the Black Death killed many in the Pale and, for a time, the area controlled by the English became smaller.

## Legal and political changes

In the Middle Ages, Parliament began to develop into the institution it is today. Its origins can be traced to the king's council of advisers, which included important noblemen and the leaders of the Church. There were few formal limits to the king's power until 1215. In that year, King John was forced by his noblemen to agree to a number of demands. The result was a charter of rights called the Magna Carta (which means the Great Charter). The Magna Carta established the idea that even the king was subject to the law. It protected the rights of the nobility and restricted the king's power to collect taxes or to make and change laws. In future, the king would need to involve his noblemen in decisions. In England, parliaments were called for the king to consult his nobles, particularly when the king needed to raise money. The numbers attending Parliament increased and two separate parts, known as Houses were established. This nobility, great landowners and bishops sat in the House of Lords. Knights, who were usually smaller landowners, and wealthy people from towns and cities were elected to sit in the House of Commons. Only a small part of the population was able to join in electing the members of the Commons. A similar Parliament developed in Scotland. It had three Houses, called Estates: the lords, the commons and the clergy. This was also a time of development in the legal system. The principle that judges are independent of the government began to be established. In England, judges developed 'common law' by a process of precedence (that is, following previous decisions) and tradition. In Scotland, the legal system developed slightly differently and laws were 'codified' (that is, written down).

## A Distinct Identity

The Middle Ages saw the development of a national culture and identity. After the Norman Conquest, the king and his noblemen had spoken Norman French and the peasants had continued to speak Anglo-Saxon. Gradually these two languages combined to become one English language. Some words in modern English – for example, 'park' and 'beauty' – are based on Norman French words. Other – for example, 'apple', 'cow' and 'summer' – are based on Anglo-Saxon words. In modern English there are often two words with very similar meanings, one from French and one from AngloSaxon. 'Demand' (French) and 'ask' (Anglo-Saxon) are examples. By 1400, in England, official documents were being written in English, and English had become the preferred language of the royal court and Parliament. In the years leading up to 1400, Geoffrey Chaucer wrote a series of poems in English about a group of people going to Canterbury on a pilgrimage. The people decided to tell each other stories on the journey, and the poems describe the travellers and some of the stories they told. This collection of poems is called The Canterbury Tales. It was one of the first books to be printed by William Caxton, the first person in England to print books using a printing press. Many of the stories are still popular. Some have been made into plays and television programmes. In Scotland, many people continued to speak Gaelic and the Scots language also developed. A number of poets began to write in the Scots language.

One example is John Barbour, who wrote The Bruce about the Battle of Bannockburn. The Middle Ages also saw a change in the type of buildings in Britain. Castles were built in many places in Britain and Ireland, partly for defence. Today many are in ruins, although some, such as Windsor and Edinburgh, are still in use. Great cathedrals – for example, Lincoln Cathedral – were also built, and many of these are still used for worship. Several of the cathedrals had windows of stained glass, telling stories about the Bible and Christian saints. The glass in York Minster is a famous example. During this period, England was an important trading nation. English wool became a very important export. People came to England from abroad to trade and also to work. Many had special skills, such as weavers from France, engineers from Germany, glass manufacturers from Italy and canal builders from Holland.

## The Wars of The Roses

In 1455, a civil war was begun to decide who should be king of England. It was fought between the supporters of two families: the House of Lancaster and the House of York. This war was called the Wars of the Roses, because the symbol of Lancaster was a red rose and the symbol of York was a white rose. The war ended with the Battle of Bosworth Field in 1485. King Richard III of the House of York was killed in the battle and Henry Tudor, the leader of the House of Lancaster, became King Henry VII. Henry then married King Richard's niece, Elizabeth of York, and united the two families. Henry was the first king of the House of Tudor. The symbol of the House of Tudor was a red rose with a white rose inside it as a sign that the Houses of York and Lancaster were now allies.

**Check that you understand**

- **The wars that took place in the Middle Ages**
- **How Parliament began to develop**
- **The way that land ownership worked**
- **The effects of the Black Death**
- **The development of English language and culture**
- **The Wars of the Roses the founding of the House of Tudor**

# The Tudors and Stuarts

After his victory in the Wars of the Roses, Henry VII wanted to make sure that England remained peaceful and that his position as king was secure. He deliberately strengthened the central administration of England and reduced the power of the nobles. He was thrifty and built up the monarchy's financial reserves. When he died, his son Henry VIII continued the policy of centralising power. Henry VIII was most famous for breaking away from the Church of Rome and marrying six times.

**The six wives of Henry VIII**

Catherine of Aragon – Catherine was a Spanish princess. She and Henry had a number of children but only one, Mary, survived. When Catherine was too old to give him another child, Henry decided to divorce her, hoping that another wife would give him a son to be his heir.

Anne Boleyn – Anne Boleyn was English. She and Henry had one daughter, Elizabeth. Anne was unpopular in the country and was accused of taking lovers. She was executed at the tower of London.

Jane Seymour – Henry married Jane after Anne's execution. She gave Henry the son he wanted, Edward, but she died shortly after his birth.

Anne of Cleves – Anne was a German princess. Henry married her for political reasons but divorced her soon after.

Catherine Howard – Catherine was a cousin of Anne Boleyn. She was also accused of taking lovers and executed.

Catherine Parr – Catherine was a widow who married Henry later in his life. She survived him and married again but died soon after.

To divorce his first wife, Henry needed the approval of the Pope. When the Pope refused, Henry established the church of England. In this new church, the king, not the Pope, would have the power to appoint bishops and order how people should worship. At the same time the Reformation was happening across Europe. This was a movement against the authority of the Pope and the ideas and practices of the Roman Catholic Church. The Protestants formed their own churches. They read the Bible in their own languages instead of Latin; they did not pray to saints or at shrines; and they believed that a person's own relationship with God was more important than submitting to the authority of the Church.

Protestant ideas gradually gained strength in England, Wales and Scotland during the 16th century. In Ireland, however, attempts by the English to impose Protestantism (alongside efforts to introduce the English system of laws about the inheritance of land) led to rebellion from the Irish chieftains, and much brutal fighting followed. During the reign of Henry VIII, Wales became formally united with England by the Act for the Government of Wales. The Welsh sent representatives to the House of Commons and the Welsh legal system was reformed. Henry VIII was succeeded by his son Edward VI, who was strongly Protestant. During his reign, the Book of Common Prayer was written to be used in the Church of England. A version of this book is still used in some churches today. Edward died at the age of 15 after ruling for just over six years, and his half-sister Mary became queen. Mary was a devout Catholic and persecuted Protestants (for this reason, she became known as 'Bloody Mary'). Mary also died after a short reign and the next monarch was her half-sister, Elizabeth, the daughter of Henry VIII and Anne Boleyn.

## Queen Elizabeth I

Queen Elizabeth I was a Protestant. She re-established the Church of England as the official Church of England. Everyone had to attend their local church and there were laws about the type of religious services and the prayers which could be said, but Elizabeth did not ask about people's real beliefs. She succeeded in finding a balance between the views of the Catholics and the more extreme Protestants. In this way, she avoided any serious religious conflict within England. Elizabeth became one of the most popular monarchs in English history, particularly after 1588, when the English defeated the Spanish Armada (a large fleet of ships), which had been sent by Spain to conquer England and restore Catholicism.

## The Reformation in Scotland and Mary, Queen of Scots

Scotland had also been strongly influenced by Protestant ideas. In 1560, the predominantly Protestant Scottish Parliament abolished the authority of the Pope in Scotland and Roman Catholic religious services became illegal. A Protestant Church of Scotland with an elected leadership was established but, unlike in England, this was not a state Church.

The queen of Scotland, Mary Stuart (often now called 'Mary, Queen of Scots') was a Catholic. She was only a week old when her father died and she became queen. Much of her childhood was spent in France. When she returned to Scotland, she was the centre of a power struggle between different groups. When her husband was murdered, Mary was suspected of involvement and fled to England. She gave her throne to her Protestant son, James

VI of Scotland. Mary was Elizabeth I's cousin and hoped that Elizabeth might help her, but Elizabeth suspected Mary of wanting to take over the English throne, and kept her prisoner for 20 years. Mary was eventually executed, accused of plotting against Elizabeth I.

## Exploration, poetry and drama

The Elizabethan period in England was a time of growing patriotism: a feeling of pride in being English, English explorers sought new trade routes and tried to expand British trade into the Spanish colonies in the Americas. Sir Francis Drake, one of the commanders in the defeat of the Spanish Armada, was one of the founders of England's naval tradition. His ship, the Golden Hind, was one of the first to sail right around ('circumnavigate') the world. In Elizabeth I's time, English settlers first began to colonise the eastern coast of America. This colonisation, particularly by people who disagreed with the religious views of the next two kings, greatly increased in the next century.

The Elizabethan period is also remembered for the richness of its poetry and drama, especially the plays and poems of William Shakespeare.

## James VI and I

Elizabeth I never married and so had no children of her own to inherit her throne. When she died in 1603 her heir was her cousin James VI of Scotland. He became King James I of England, Wales and Ireland but Scotland remained a separate country.

## The King James Bible

One achievement of King James' reign was a new translation of the Bible into English. This translation is known as the 'King James Version' or the 'Authorised Version'. It was not the first English Bible but is a version which continues to be used in many Protestant churches today.

# Ireland

During this period, Ireland was an almost completely Catholic country. Henry VII and Henry VIII had extended English control outside the Pale and had established English authority over the whole country. Henry VIII took the title 'King of Ireland'. English laws were introduced and local leaders were expected to follow the instructions of the Lord Lieutenants in Dublin. During the reigns of Elizabeth I and James I, many people in Ireland opposed rule by the Protestant government in England. There were a number of rebellions. The English government encouraged Scottish and English Protestants to settle in Ulster, the northern province of Ireland, taking over the land from Catholic landholders. These settlements were known as plantations. Many of the new settlers came from south-west Scotland and other land was given to companies based in London. James later organised similar plantations in several other parts of Ireland. This had serious longterm consequence for the history of England, Scotland and Ireland.

# The Rise of Parliament

Elizabeth I was very skilled at managing Parliament. During her reign, she was successful in balancing her wishes and views against those of the House of Lords and those of the House of Commons, which was increasingly Protestant in its views. James I and his son Charles I were less skilled politically. Both believed in the 'Divine Right of Kings': the idea that the king was directly appointed by God to rule. They thought that the king should be able to act without having to seek approval from Parliament. When Charles I inherited the thrones of England, Wales, Ireland and Scotland, he tried to rule in line with this principle. When he could not get Parliament to agree with his religious and foreign policies, he tried to rule without the Parliament at all. For 11 years, he found ways in which to raise money without Parliament's approval but eventually trouble in Scotland meant that he had to recall Parliament.

## The beginning of the English Civil War

Charles I wanted the worship of the Church of England to include more ceremony and introduced a revise Prayer Book. He tried to impose this Prayer Book on the Presbyterian Church in Scotland and this led to serious unrest. A Scottish army was formed and Charles could not find the money he needed for his own army without the help of Parliament. In 1640, he recalled Parliament to ask it for funds. Many in Parliament were Puritans, a group of Protestants who advocated strict and simple religious doctrine and worship. They did not agree with the king's religious views and disliked his reforms of the Church of England. Parliament refused to give the king the money he asked for, even after the Scottish army invaded England.

Another rebellion began in Ireland because the Roman Catholics in Ireland were afraid of the growing power of the Puritans. Parliament took this opportunity to demand control of the English army – a change that would have transferred substantial power from the king to Parliament. In response, Charles I entered the House of Commons and tried to arrest five parliamentary leaders, but they had been warned and were not there. (No monarch has set foot in the Commons since.) Civil war between the king and Parliament could not now be avoided and began in 1642. The country spilt into those who supported the king (the Cavaliers) and those who supported Parliament (the Roundheads).

## Oliver Cromwell & The English Republic

The king's army was defeated at the Battles of Marston Moor and Naseby. By 1646, it was clear that the Parliament had won the war. Charles was held prisoner by the parliamentary army. He was still unwilling to reach any agreement with the Parliament and in 1649 he was executed. England declared itself a republic, called the Commonwealth. It no longer had a monarch. For a time, it was not totally clear how the country would be governed. For now, the army was in control. One of its generals, Oliver Cromwell, was sent to Ireland, where the revolt which had begun in 1641 still continued and where there was still a Royalist army. Cromwell was successful in establishing the authority of the English Parliament but did this with such violence that even today Cromwell remains a controversial figure in Ireland. The Scots had not agreed to the execution of Charles I and declared his son Charles II to be king. He was crowned king of Scotland and led a Scottish army into England. Cromwell defeated this army in the Battles of Dunbar and Worcester. Charles II escaped from Worcester, famously hiding in an oak tree on one occasion, and eventually fled to Europe. Parliament now controlled Scotland as well as England and Wales. After his campaign in Ireland and victory over Charles II at Worcester, Cromwell was recognised as the leader of the new republic. He was given the title of Lord Protector and ruled until his death in 1658. When Cromwell died, his son, Richard, became Lord Protector in his place but was not able to control the army or the government. Although Britain had been a republic for 11 years, without Oliver Cromwell there was no clear leader or system of government. Many people in the country wanted stability. People began to talk about the need for a king.

# The Restoration

In May 1660, Parliament invited Charles II to come back from exile in The Netherlands. He was crowned King Charles II of England, Wales, Scotland and Ireland. Charles II made it clear that he had 'no wish to go on his travels again'. He understood that he could not always do as he wished but would sometimes need to reach agreement with the Parliament. Generally, Parliament supported his policies. The Church of England again became the established official Church. Both Roman Catholics and Puritans were kept out of power. During Charles II's reign, in 1665, there was a major outbreak of plague in London. Thousands of people died, especially in poorer areas. The following year, a great fire destroyed much of the city, including many churches and St Paul's Cathedral. London was rebuilt with a new St Paul's, which was designed by a famous architect, Sir Christopher Wren. Samuel Pepys wrote about these events in a diary which was later published and is still read today.

The Habeas Corpus Act became law in 1679. This was a very important piece of legislation which remains relevant today. Habeas corpus is Latin for 'you must present the person in court'. The Act guaranteed that no one could be held prisoner unlawfully. Every prisoner has a right to a court hearing. Charles II was interested in science. During his reign, the Royal Society was formed to promote 'natural knowledge'. This is the oldest surviving scientific society in the world. Among its early members were Sir Edmund Halley who successfully predicted the return of the comet now called Halley's Comet, and Sir Isaac Newton.

## Isaac Newton (1643-1727)

Born in Lincolnshire, eastern England, Isaac Newton first became interested in science when he studied at Cambridge University. He became an important figure in the field. His most famous published work was Philosophiae Naturalis Principia Mathematica ('Mathematical Principle of Natural Philosophy'), which showed how gravity applied to the whole universe. Newton also discovered that white light is made up of the colours of the rainbow. Many of his discoveries are still important for modern science.

## A Catholic king

Charles II had no legitimate children. He died in 1685 and his brother, James, who was a Roman Catholic, became King James II in England, Wales and Ireland and King James VII of Scotland. James favoured Roman Catholics and allowed them to be army officers, which an Act of Parliament had forbidden. He did not seek to reach agreements with Parliament and arrested some of the bishops of the Church of England. People in England worried that James wanted to make England a Catholic country once more. However, his heirs were his two daughters, who were both firmly Protestant, and people thought that this meant there would soon be a Protestant monarch again. Then James's wife had a son. Suddenly, it seemed likely that the next monarch would not be a Protestant after all.

## The Glorious Revolution

James II's elder daughter, Mary, was married to her cousin William of Orange, the Protestant ruler of the Netherlands. In 1688, important Protestants in England asked William to invade England and proclaim himself king. When William reached England, there was no resistance. James fled to France and William took over the throne, becoming William III in England, Wales and Ireland, and William II of Scotland. William ruled jointly with Mary. This event was later called the 'Glorious Revolution' because there was no fighting in England and because it guaranteed the power of Parliament, ending the threat of monarch ruling on his or her own as he or she wished. James II wanted to regain the throne and invaded Ireland with the help of a French army. William defeated James II at the Battle of the Boyne in Ireland in 1690, an event which is still celebrated by some in Northern Ireland today. William re-conquered Ireland and James fled back to France. Many restrictions were placed on the Roman Catholic Church in Ireland and Irish Catholics were unable to take part in the government. There was also support for James in Scotland. An attempt at an armed rebellion in support of James was quickly defeated at Killiecrankie. All Scottish clans were required formally to accept William as king by taking an oath. The MacDonalds of Glencoe were late in taking an oath. The memory of this massacre meant some Scots distrusted the new government. Some continued to believe that James was the rightful king, particularly in Scotland. Some joined him in exile in France; others were secret supporters. James' supporters became known as Jacobites.

**Check that you understand**

• **How and why religion changed during this period**
• **The importance of poetry and drama in the Elizabethan period**
• **About the involvement of Britain in Ireland**
• **The development of Parliament and the only period in history when England was a republic • Why there was a restoration of the monarchy**
• **How the Glorious Revolution happened**

# Constitutional monarchy – the Bill of Rights

At the coronation of William and Mary, a Declaration of Rights was read. This confirmed that the king would no longer be able to raise taxes and administer justice without agreement from

Parliament. The balance of power between monarch and Parliament had now permanently changed. The Bill of Rights, 1689, confirmed the rights of Parliament and the limits of the king's power. Parliament took control of who could be monarch and declared that the king or queen must be a Protestant. A new Parliament had to be elected at least every three years (later this became seven years and now it is five years). Every year the monarch had to ask Parliament to renew funding for the army and the navy. These changes meant that, to be able to govern effectively, the monarch needed to have advisers, or ministers, who would be able to ensure a majority of votes in the House of Commons and the House of Lords. There were two main groups in Parliament, known as the Whigs and the Tories. (The modern Conservative Party is still sometimes referred to as the Tories.) This was the beginning of party politics. This was also an important time for the development of a free press (newspapers and other publications which are not controlled by the government). From 1695, newspapers were allowed to operate without a government licence. Increasing numbers of newspapers began to be published. The laws passed after the Glorious Revolution are the beginning of what is called 'constitutional monarchy'. The monarch remained very important but was no longer able to insist on particular policies or actions if Parliament did not agree. After William III, the ministers gradually became more important than the monarch but this was not a democracy in the modern sense. The number of people who had the right to vote for members of Parliament was still very small. Only men who owned property of a certain value were able to vote. No women at all had the vote. Some constituencies were controlled by a single wealthy family. They were called the 'pocket boroughs'. Other constituencies had hardly any voters and were called 'rotten boroughs'.

## A Growing Population

This was a time when many people left Britain and Ireland to settle in new colonies in America and elsewhere, but others came to live in Britain. The first Jews to come to Britain since the Middle Ages settled in London in 1656. Between 1680 and 1720 many refugees called Huguenots came from France. They were Protestants and had been persecuted for their religion. Many were educated and skilled and worked as scientists, in banking, or in weaving or other crafts.

## The Act or Treaty of Union in Scotland

William and Mary's successor, Queen Anne, had no surviving children. This created uncertainty over the succession in England, Wales and Ireland and in Scotland. The Act of Union, known as the Treaty of Union in Scotland, was therefore agreed in 1707, creating the Kingdom of Great Britain. Although Scotland was no longer an independent country, it kept its own legal and education systems and Presbyterian Church.

## The Prime Minister

When Queen Anne died in 1714, Parliament chose a German, George I, to be the next king, because he was Anne's nearest Protestant relative. An attempt by Scottish Jacobites to put James II's son on the throne instead was quickly defeated. George I did not speak very good English and this increased his need to rely on his ministers. The most important minister in Parliament became known as the Prime Minister. The first man to be called this was Sir Robert Walpole, who was Prime Minister from 1721 to 1742.

## The rebellion of the clans

In 1745 there was another attempt to put a Stuart king back on the throne in place of George I's son, George II. Charles Edward Stuart (Bonnie Prince Charlie), the grandson of James II, landed in Scotland. He was supported by clansmen from the Scottish highlands and raised an army. Charles initially had some successes but was defeated by George II's army at the Battle of Culloden in 1746. Charles escaped back to Europe. The clans lost a lot of their power and influence after Culloden. Chieftains became landlords if they had the favour of the English king, and clansmen became tenants who had to pay for the land they used. A process began which became known as the 'Highland Clearances'. Many Scottish landlords destroyed individual small farms (known as 'crofts') to make space for large flocks of sheep and cattle. Evictions became very common in the early 19th century. Many Scottish people left for North America at this time.

## Robert Burns (1759-96)

Known in Scotland as 'The Bard', Robert Burns was a Scottish poet. He wrote in the Scots language, English with some Scottish words and standard English. He also revised a lot of the traditional folk songs by changing or adding lyrics. Burns' best-known work is probably the song Auld Lang Syne, which is sung by people in the UK and other countries when they are celebrating the New Year (or Hogmanay as it is called in Scotland).

# The Enlightenment

During the 18th century, new ideas about politics, philosophy and science were developed. This is often called 'the Enlightenment'. Many of the great thinkers of the Enlightenment were Scottish. Adam Smith developed ideas about economics which are still referred to today. David Hume's ideas about human nature continue to influence philosophers. Scientific discoveries, such as James Watt's work on steam power, helped the progress of the Industrial Revolution. One of the most important principles of the Enlightenment was that everyone should have the right to their own political and religious beliefs and that the state should not try to dictate to them. This continues to be an important principle in the UK today.

# The Industrial Revolution

Before the 18th century, agriculture was the biggest source of employment in Britain. There were many cottage industries, where people worked from home to produce goods such as cloth and lace. The Industrial Revolution was the rapid development of industry in Britain in the 18th and 19th centuries. Britain was the first country to industrialise on a large scale. It happened because of the development of machinery and the use of steam power. Agriculture and the manufacturing of goods became mechanised. This made things more efficient and increased production. Coal and other raw materials were needed to power the new factories. Many people moved from the countryside and started working in the mining and manufacturing industries. The development of the Bessemer process for the mass production of steel led to the development of the shipbuilding industry and the railways. Manufacturing jobs became the main source of employment in Britain.

Better transport links were needed to transport raw materials and manufactured goods. Canals were built to link the factories to towns and cities and to the ports, particularly in the new industrial areas in the middle and north of England. Working conditions during the Industrial Revolution were very poor. There were no laws to protect employees, who were often forced to work long hours in dangerous situations. Children also worked and were treated in the same way as adults. Sometimes they were treated even more harshly.

This was also a time of increased colonisation overseas. Captain James Cook mapped the coast of Australia and a few colonies were established there. Britain gained control over Canada, and the East India Company, originally set up to trade, gained control of large parts of India. Colonies began to be established in southern Africa. Britain traded all over the world and began to import more goods. Sugar and tobacco came from North America and the west Indies; textiles, tea and spices came from India and the area that is today called Indonesia. Trading and settlements overseas sometimes brought Britain into conflict with other countries, particularly France, which was expanding and trading in a similar way in many of the same areas of the world.

## Richard Arkwright (1732-92)

Born in 1732, Arkwright originally trained and worked as a barber. He was able to dye hair and make wigs. When wigs became less popular, he started to work in textiles. He improved the original carding machine. Carding is the process of preparing fibres for spinning into yarn and fabric. He also developed horse-driven spinning mills that used only one machine. This increased the efficiency of production. Later, he used the steam engine to power machinery. Arkwright is particularly remembered for the efficient and profitable way that he ran his factories.

## Sake Dean Mahomet (1759-1851)

Mahomet was born is 1759 and grew up in the Bengal region of India. He served in the Bengal army and came to Britain in 1782. He then moved to Ireland and eloped with an Irish girl called Jane Daly in 1786, returning to England at the turn of the century. In 1810 he opened the Hindoostane Coffee House in George Street, London. It was the first curry house to open in Britain. Mahomet and his wife also introduced 'shampooing', the Indian art of head massage, to Britain.

# The slave trade

BAND OF CAPTIVES DRIVEN INTO SLAVERY

This commercial expansion and prosperity was sustained in part by the booming slave trade. While slavery was illegal within Britain itself, by the 18th century it was a fully established overseas industry, dominated by Britain and the American colonies. Slaves came primarily from West Africa. Travelling on British ships in horrible conditions, they were taken to America and the Caribbean, where they were made to work on tobacco and sugar plantations. The living and working conditions for slaves were very bad. Many slaves tried to escape and others revolted against their owners in protest at their terrible treatment.

There were, however people in Britain who opposed the slave trade. The first formal anti-slavery groups were set up by the Quakers in the late 1700s, and they petitioned Parliament to ban the practice. William Wilberforce, an evangelical Christian and a member of Parliament, also played an important part in changing the law. Along with other abolitionists (people who supported the abolition of slavery), he succeeded in turning public opinion against the slave trade. In 1807, it became illegal to trade slaves in British ships or from British ports, and in 1833 the Emancipation Act abolished slavery throughout the British Empire. The Royal Navy stopped slave ships from other countries, freed the slaves and punished the slave traders. After 1833, 2 million Indian and Chinese workers were employed to replace the freed slaves. They worked on sugar plantations in the Caribbean, in mines in South Africa, on railways in East Africa and in the army in Kenya.

# The American War of Independence

By the 1760s, there were substantial British colonies in North America. The colonies were wealthy and largely in control of their own affairs. Many of the colonist families had originally gone to North America in order to have religious freedom. They were well educated and interested in ideas of liberty. The British government wanted to tax the colonies. The colonists saw this as an attack on their freedom and said there should be 'no taxation without representation' in the British Parliament. Parliament tried to compromise by repealing some of the taxes, but relationships between the British government and the colonies continued to worsen. Fighting broke out between the colonists and the British forces. In 1776, 13 American colonies declared their independence, stating that people had a right to establish their own governments. The colonists eventually defeated the British army and Britain recognised the colonies' independence in 1783.

## War with France

During the 18th century, Britain fought a number of wars with France. In 1789, there was a revolution in France and the new French government soon declared war on Britain. Napoleon, who became Emperor of France, continued the war. Britain's navy fought against combined French and Spanish fleets, winning the Battle of Trafalgar in 1805. Admiral Nelson was in charge of the British fleet at Trafalgar and was killed in the battle. Nelson's Column in Trafalgar Square, London, is a monument to him. His ship, HMS Victory, can be visited in Portsmouth. The British army also fought against the French. In 1815, the French Wars ended with the defeat of the Emperor Napoleon by the Duke of Wellington at the Battle of Waterloo. Wellington was known as the Iron Duke and later became Prime Minister.

## The Union Flag

Although Ireland has had the same monarch as England and Wales since Henry VIII, it had remained a separate country. In 1801, Ireland became unified with England, Scotland and Wales after the Act of Union of 1800. This created the United Kingdom of Great Britain and Ireland. One symbol of this union between England, Scotland, Wales and Ireland was a new version of the official flag, the Union Flag. This is still used today as the official flag of the UK.

The Union Flag consists of three crosses:

• This cross of St George, patron saint of England, is a red cross on a white ground.
• The cross of St Andrew, patron saint of Scotland, is a diagonal white cross on a blue ground.
• The cross of St Patrick, patron saint of Ireland, is a diagonal red cross on a white ground.

# The Victorian Age

In 1837, Queen Victoria became queen of the UK at the age of 18. She reigned until 1901, almost 64 years. At the date of writing (2013) this is the longest reign of any British monarch. Her reign is known as the Victorian Age. It was a time when Britain increased in power and influence abroad. Within the UK, the middle classes became increasingly significant and a number of reformers led moves to improve conditions of life for the poor.

During the Victorian period, the British Empire grew to cover all of India, Australia and large parts of Africa. It became the largest empire the world has ever seen, with an estimated population of more than 400 million people. Many people were encouraged to leave the UK to settle overseas. Between 1853 and 1913, as many as 13 million British citizens left the country. People continued to come to Britain from other parts of the world. For example, between 1870 and 1914, around 120, 000 Russian and Polish Jews came to Britain to escape persecution. Many settled in London's East End and in Manchester and Leeds. People from the Empire, including India and Africa, also came to Britain to live, work and study.

# Trade and industry

Britain continued to be a great trading nation. The government began to promote policies of free trade, abolishing a number of taxes on imported goods. One example of this was the repealing of the Corn Laws in 1846. These had prevented the import of cheap grain. The reforms helped the development of the British industry, because raw materials could now be imported cheaply. Working conditions in factories gradually became better. In 1847, the number of hours that women and children could work was limited by law to 10 hours per day. Better housing began to be built for workers. Transport links also improved, enabling goods and people to move more easily around the country. Just before Victoria came to the throne, the father and son George and Robert Stephenson pioneered the railway engine and a major expansion of the railways took place in the Victorian period. Railways were built throughout the Empire. There were also great advances in other areas, such as the building of bridges by engineers such as Isambard Kingdom Brunel. British industry led the world in the 19th century. The UK produced more than half of the world's iron, coal and cotton cloth. The UK also became a centre for financial services, including insurance and banking. In 1851, the Great Exhibition opened in Hyde Park in the Crystal Palace, a huge building made of steel and glass. Exhibits ranged from huge machines to handmade goods. Countries from all over the world showed their goods but most of the objects were made in Britain.

## Isambard Kingdom Brunel (1806-59)

Brunel was originally from Portsmouth, England. He was an engineer who built tunnels, bridges, railway lines and ships. He was responsible for constructing the Great Western Railway, which was the first major railway built in Britain. It runs from Paddington Station in London to the south west of England, the West Midlands and Wales. Many of Brunel's bridges are still in use today.

## The Crimean War

From 1853 to 1856, Britain fought with Turkey and France against Russia in the Crimean War. It was the first war to be extensively covered by the media through news stories and photographs. The conditions were very poor and many soldiers died from illnesses they caught in the hospitals, rather than from war wounds. Queen Victoria introduced the Victoria Cross medal during this war. It honours acts of valour by soldiers.

## Florence Nightingale (1820-1910)

Florence Nightingale was born in Italy to English parents. At the age of 31, she trained as a nurse in Germany. In 1854, she went to Turkey and worked in military hospitals, treating soldiers who were fighting in the Crimean War. She and her fellow nurses improved the conditions in the hospital and reduced the mortality rate. In 1860 she established the Nightingale Training School for nurses at St Thomas' Hospital in London. The school was the first of its kind and still exists today, as do many of the practices that Florence used. She is often regarded as the founder of modern nursing. Ireland in the 19th century Conditions in Ireland were not as good as in the rest of the UK. Two-thirds of the population still depended on farming to make their living, often on very small plots of land. In the middle of the century the potato crop failed, and Ireland suffered a famine. A million people died from disease and starvation. Another million and a half left Ireland. Some emigrated to the United States and others came to England. By 1861 there were large populations of Irish people in cities such as Liverpool, London, Manchester and Glasgow. The Irish Nationalist movement had grown strongly through the 19th century. Some, such as the Fenians, favoured complete independence. Others, such as Charles Stuart Parnell, advocated 'Home Rule', in which Ireland would remain in the UK but have its own parliament.

# The right to vote

As the middle classes in the wealthy industrial towns and cities grew in influence, they began to demand more political power. The Reform Act of 1832 had greatly increased the number of people with the right to vote. The act also abolished the old pocket and rotten boroughs and more parliamentary seats were given to the towns and cities. There was a permanent shift of political power from the countryside to the towns but voting was still based on ownership of the property. This meant that members of the working class were still unable to vote.

A movement began to demand the vote for the working classes and other people without property. Campaigners, called the Chartists, presented petitions to Parliament. At first they seemed to be unsuccessful, but in 1867 there was another Reform Act. This created many more urban seats in Parliament and reduced the amount of property that people needed to have before they could vote. However, the majority of men still did not have the right to vote and no women could vote. Politicians realised that the increased number of voters meant that they needed to persuade people to vote for them if they were to be sure of being elected to Parliament. The political parties began to create organisations to reach out to ordinary voters. Universal suffrage (the right of every adult, male or female, to vote) followed in the next century. In common with the rest of Europe, women in 19th century Britain had fewer rights than men. Until 1870, when a woman got married, her earnings, property and money automatically belonged to her husband. Acts of Parliament in 1870 and 1882 gave wives the right to keep their own earnings and property. In the late 19th and early 20th centuries, an increasing number of women campaigned and demonstrated for greater rights and, in particular, the right to vote. They formed the women's suffrage movement and became known as the 'suffragettes'.

## Emmeline Pankhurst (1858-1928)

Emmeline Pankhurst was born in Manchester in 1858. She set up the women's Franchise League in 1889, which fought to get the vote in local elections for married women. In 1903 she helped found the Women's Social and Political Union (WSPU). This was the first group whose members were called 'suffragettes'. The group used civil disobedience as part of their protest to gain the vote for women. They chained themselves to railings, smashed windows and committed arson. Many of the women, including Emmeline, went on a hunger strike. In 1918, women over the age of 30 were given voting rights and the right to stand for Parliament, partly in recognition of the contribution women made to the war effort during the First World War. Shortly before Emmeline's death in 1928, women were given the right to vote at the age of 21, the same as men.

## The future of the Empire

Although the British Empire continued to grow until the 1920s, there was already discussion in the late 19th century about its future direction. Supporters of expansion believed that the Empire benefited Britain through increased trade and commerce. Others thought the Empire had become over-expanded and that the frequent conflicts in many parts of the Empire, such as India's north-west frontier or southern Africa, were a drain on resources. Yet the great majority of British people believed in the Empire as a force for good in the world.

The Boer War of 1899 to 1902 made the discussions about the future of the Empire more urgent. The British went to war in South Africa with settlers from the Netherlands called the Boers. The Boers fought fiercely and the war went on for over three years. Many died in the fighting and many more from disease. There was some public sympathy for the Boers and people began to question whether the Empire could continue. As different parts of the Empire developed, they won greater freedom and autonomy from Britain. Eventually, by the second half of the 20th century, there was, for the most part, an orderly transition from Empire to Commonwealth, with countries being granted their independence.

# Rudyard Kipling (1865-1936)

Rudyard Kipling was born in India in 1865 and later lived in India, the UK and the USA. He wrote books and poems set in both India and the UK. His poems and novels reflected the idea that the British Empire was a force for good. Kipling was awarded the Nobel Prize in Literature in 1907. His books include the Just So Stories and The Jungle Book, which continue to be popular today. His poem If has often been voted among the UK's favourite poems. It begins with these words: 'If you can keep your head when all about you are losing theirs and blaming it on you; If you can trust yourself when all men doubt you, But make allowance for their doubting too; If you can wait and not be tired by waiting, or being lied about, don't deal in lies, or being hated, don't give way to hating, And yet don't look too good, nor talk too wise' (If, Rudyard Kipling).

**Check that you understand**

- **The change in the balance of power between Parliament and the monarchy**
- **When and why Scotland joined England and Wales to become Great Britain**
- **The reasons for a rebellion in Scotland led by Bonnie Prince Charlie**
- **The ideas of the Enlightenment**
- **The importance of the Industrial Revolution and development of industry**
- **The slave trade and when it was abolished**
- **The growth of the British Empire • How democracy developed during this period**

# The First World War

The early 20th century was a time of optimism in Britain. The nation, with its expansive Empire, well-admired navy, thriving industry and strong political institutions, was what is now known as a global 'superpower'. It was also a time of social progress. Financial help for the unemployed, old-age pensions and free school meals were just a few of the important measures introduced. Various laws were passed to improve safety in the workplace; town planning rules were tightened to prevent the further development of slums; and better support was given to mothers and their children after divorce or separation. Local government became more democratic and a salary for members of Parliament (MPs) was introduced for the first time, making it easier for more people to take part in public life.

This era of optimism and progress was cut short when war broke out between several European nations. On 28 June 1914, Archduke Franz Ferdinand of Austria was assassinated. This set off a chain of events leading to the First World War (1914-18). But while the assassination provided the trigger for war, other factors – such as a growing sense of nationalism in many European states; increasing militarism; imperialism; and the division of the major European powers into two camps – all set the conditions for war. The conflict was centred in Europe, but it was a global war involving nations from around the world. Britain was part of the Allied Powers, which included (amongst others) France, Russia, Japan, Belgium, Serbia – and later, Greece, Italy, Romania and the United States.

The whole of the British Empire was involved in the conflict – for example, more than a million Indians fought on behalf of Britain in lots of different countries, and around 40, 000 were killed. Men from the West Indies, Africa, Australia, New Zealand and Canada also fought with the British. The Allies fought against the Central Powers – mainly Germany, the Austro-Hungarian Empire, the Ottoman Empire and later Bulgaria. Millions of people were killed or wounded, with more than 2 million British casualties. One battle, the British attack of the Somme in July 1916, resulted in about 60,000 British casualties on the first day alone.

The First World War ended at 11.00 am on 11th November 1918 with victory for Britain and its allies.

# The partition of Ireland

In 1913, the British government promised 'Home Rule' for Ireland. The proposal was to have a self-governing Ireland with its own parliament but still part of the UK. A Home Rule Bill was introduced in Parliament. It was opposed by the Protestants in the north of Ireland, who threatened to resist Home Rule by force. The outbreak of the First World War led the British government to postpone any changes in Ireland. Irish Nationalists were not willing to wait and in 1916 there was an uprising (the Easter Rising) against the British in Dublin. The leaders of the uprising were executed under military law. A guerrilla war against the British army and the police in Ireland followed. In 1921 a peace treaty was signed and in 1922 Ireland became two countries. The six countries in the north which were mainly Protestant remained part of the UK under the name Northern Ireland. The rest of Ireland became the Irish Free State. It had its own government and became a republic in 1949. There were people in both parts of Ireland who disagree with the split between the North and the South. They still wanted Ireland to be one independent country. Years of disagreement led to a terror campaign in Northern Ireland and elsewhere. The conflict between those wishing for full Irish independence and those wishing to remain loyal to the British government is often referred to as 'the Troubles'.

## The inter-war period

In the 1920s, many people's living conditions got better. There were improvements in public housing and new homes were built in many towns and cities. However, in 1929, the world entered the 'Great Depression' and some parts of the UK suffered mass unemployment. The effects of the depression of the 1930s were felt differently in different parts of the UK. The traditional heavy industries such as shipbuilding were badly affected but new industries – including the automobile and aviation industries – developed. As prices generally fell, those in work had more money to spend. Car ownership doubled from 1 million to 2 million between 1930 and 1939. In addition, many new houses were built. It was also a time of cultural blossoming, with writers such as Graham Greene and Evelyn Waugh prominent. The economist John Maynard Keynes published influential new theories of economics. The BBC started radio broadcasts in 1922 and began the world's first regular television service in 1936.

# The Second World War

Adolf Hitler came to power in Germany in 1933. He believed that the conditions imposed on Germany by the Allies after the First World War were unfair; he also wanted to conquer more land for the German people. He set about renegotiating treaties, building up arms, and testing Germany's military strength in nearby countries. The British government tried to avoid another war. However, when Hitler invaded Poland in 1939, Britain and France declared war in order to stop his aggression. The war was initially fought between the Axis powers (fascist Germany and Italy and the Empire of Japan) and the Allies. The main countries on the allied side were the UK, France, Poland, Australia, New Zealand, Canada, and the Union of South Africa. Having occupied Austria and invaded Czechoslovakia, Hitler followed his invasion of Poland by taking control of Belgium and the Netherlands. Then, in 1940, German forces defeated allied troops and advanced through France. At this time of national crisis, Winston Churchill became Prime Minister and Britain's war leader.

As France fell, the British decided to evacuate British and French solders from France in a huge naval operation. Many civilian volunteers in small pleasure and fishing boats from Britain helped the Navy to rescue more than 300,000 men from the beaches around Dunkirk. Although many lives and a lot of equipment were lost, the evacuation was a success and meant that Britain was better able to continue the fight against the Germans.

The evacuation gave rise to the phrase 'the Dunkirk spirit'. From the end of June 1940 until the German invasion of the Soviet Union in June 1941, Britain and the Empire stood almost alone against Nazi Germany. Hitler wanted to invade Britain, but before sending in troops, Germany needed to control the air campaign against Britain, but the British resisted with their fighter planes and eventually won the crucial aerial battle against the Germans, called 'the Battle of Britain', in the summer of 1940. The most important planes used by the Royal Air Force in the Battle of Britain were the Spitfire and the Hurricane – which were designed and built in Britain.

Despite this crucial victory, the German air force was able to continue bombing London and other British cities at night-time. This was called the Blitz. Coventry was almost totally destroyed and a great deal of damage was done in other cities, especially in the East End of London. Despite the destruction, there was a strong national spirit of resistance in the UK. The phrase 'the Blitz spirit' is still used today to describe Britons pulling together in the face of adversity. At the same time as defending Britain, the British military was fighting the Axis on many other fronts. In Singapore, the Japanese defeated the British and then occupied Burma, threatening India. The United States entered the war when the Japanese bombed its naval base at Pearl Harbor in December 1941.

That same year, Hitler attempted the largest invasion in history by attacking the Soviet Union. It was a fierce conflict, with huge losses on both sides. German forces were ultimately repelled by the Soviets, and the damage they sustained proved to be a pivotal point in the war. The allied forces gradually gained the upper hand, winning significant victories in North Africa and Italy. German losses in the Soviet Union, combined with the support of the Americans, meant that the Allies were eventually strong enough to attack Hitler's forces in Western Europe. On 6 June 1944, allied forces landed in Normandy (this event is often referred to as 'D-Day'). Following victory on the beaches of Normandy, the allied forces pressed on through France and eventually into Germany. The Allies comprehensively defeated Germany in May 1945.

The war against Japan ended in August 1945 when the United States dropped its newly developed atom bombs on the Japanese cities of Hiroshima and Nagasaki. Scientists led by Ernest Rutherford, working at Manchester and then Cambridge University, were the first to 'split the atom' and took part in the Manhattan Project in the United States, which developed the atomic bomb. The war was finally over.

# Winston Churchill (1874-1965)

Churchill was the son of a politician and, before becoming a Conservative MP in 1900, was a soldier and journalist. In May 1940 he became Prime Minister. He refused to surrender to the Nazis and was an inspirational leader to the British people in a time of hardship. He lost the General Election in 1945 but returned as Prime Minister in 1951. He was an MP until he stood down at the 1964 General Election. Following his death in 1965, he was given a state funeral. He remains a much admired figure to this day, and in 2002 was voted the greatest Briton of all time by the public. During the War, he made many famous speeches including lines which you may still hear: 'I have nothing to offer but blood, toil, tears and sweat' Churchill's first speech to the House of Commons after he became Prime Minister, 1940 'We shall fight on the beaches, we shall fight on the landing grounds, we shall fight in the fields and in the streets, we shall fight in the hills; we shall never surrender'.

## Alexander Fleming (1881-1955)

Born in Scotland, Fleming moved to London as a teenager and later qualified as a doctor. He was researching influenza (the 'flu') in 1928 when he discovered penicillin. This was then further developed into a usable drug by the scientists Howard Florey and Ernst Chain. By the 1940s it was in mass production. Fleming won the Nobel Prize in Medicine in 1945. Penicillin is still used to treat bacterial infections today.

**Check that you understand**
• **What happened during the First World War**
• **The partition of Ireland and the establishment of the UK as it is today**
• **The events of the Second World War**

## The Welfare State

Although the UK had won the war, the country was exhausted economically and the people wanted change. During the war, there had been significant reforms to the educational system and people now looked for wider social reforms. In 1945 the British people elected a Labour government. The new Prime Minister was Clement Attlee, who promised to introduce the welfare state outlined in the Beveridge Report. In 1948, Aneurin (Nye) Bevan, the Minister for Health, led the establishment of the National Health Service (NHS), which guaranteed a minimum standard of health care for all, free at the point of use. A national system of benefits was also introduced to provide 'social security', so that the population would be protected from the 'cradle to the grave'.

The government took into public ownership (nationalised) the railways, coal mines and gas, water and electricity supplies. Another aspect of change was self-government for former colonies. In 1947, independence was granted to nine countries, including India, Pakistan and Ceylon (now Sri Lanka). Other colonies in Africa, the Caribbean and the Pacific achieved independence over the next 20 years.

The UK developed its own atomic bomb and joined the new North Atlantic Treaty Organization (NATO), an alliance of nations set up to resist the perceived threat of invasion by the Soviet Union and it allies. Britain had a Conservative government from 1951 to 1964. The 1950s were a period of economic recovery after the war and increasing prosperity for working people. The Prime Minister of the day, Harold Macmillan, was famous for his 'wind of change' speech about decolonisation and independence for the countries of the Empire.

## Clement Attlee (1883-1967)

Clement Attlee was born in London in 1883. His father was a solicitor and, after studying at Oxford University, Attlee became a barrister. He gave this up to do social work in East London and eventually became a Labour MP. He was Winston Churchill's Deputy Prime Minister in the wartime coalition government and became Prime Minister after the Labour Party won the 1945 election. He was Prime Minister from 1945 to 1951 and led the Labour Party for 20 years. Attlee's government undertook the nationalisation of major industries (like coal and steel), created the National Health Service and implemented many of Beveridge's plans for a stronger welfare state. Attlee also introduced measures to improve the conditions of workers.

## William Beveridge (1879-1963)

William Beveridge (later Lord Beveridge) was a British economist and reformer. He served briefly as a Liberal MP and was subsequently the leader of the Liberals in the House of Lords but is best known for the 1942 report Social Insurance and Allied Services (known as the Beveridge Report). The report was commissioned by the wartime government in 1941. It recommended that the government should find ways of fighting the five 'Giant Evils' of Want, Disease, Ignorance, Squalor and Idleness and provided the basis of the modern welfare state.

## R A Butler (1902-82)

Richard Austen Butler (later Lord Butler) was born in 1902. He became a Conservative MP in 1923 and held several positions before becoming responsible for education in 1941. In this role, he oversaw the introduction of the Education Act 1944 (often called 'The Butler Act'), which introduced free secondary education in England and Wales. The education system has changed significantly since the Act was introduced, but the division between primary and secondary schools that it enforced still remains in most areas of Britain.

# Dylan Thomas (1914-53)

Dylan Thomas was a Welsh poet and writer. He often read and performed his work in public, including for the BBC. His most well-known works include the radio play Under Milk Wood, first performed after his death in 1954, and the poem Do Not Go Gentle into That Good Night, which he wrote for his dying father in 1952. He died at the age of 39 in New York. There are several memorials to him in his birthplace, Swansea, including a statue and the Dylan Thomas Centre.

# Migration in Post-war Britain

Rebuilding Britain after the Second World War was a huge task. There were labour shortages and the British government encouraged workers from Ireland and other parts of Europe to come to the UK and help with the reconstruction. In 1948, people from the West Indies were also invited to come and work.

During the 1950s, there was still a shortage of labour in the UK. Further immigration was therefore encouraged for economic reasons, and many industries advertised for workers from overseas. For example, centres were set up in the West Indies to recruit people to drive buses. Textile and engineering firms from the north of England and the Midlands sent agents to India and Pakistan to find workers. For about 25 years, people from the West Indies, India, Pakistan and (later) Bangladesh travelled to work and settle in Britain.

## Social change in the 1960s

The decade of the 1960s was a period of significant social change. It was known as the 'swinging sixties'. There was growth in British fashion, cinema and popular music. Two well-known pop music groups at the time were The Beatles and The Rolling Stones. People started to become better off and many bought cars and other consumer goods. It was also a time when social laws were liberalised, for example in relation to divorce and to abortion in England, Wales and Scotland. The position of women in the workplace also improved. It was quite common at the time for employers to ask women to leave their jobs when they got married, but Parliament passed new laws giving women the right to equal pay and made it illegal for employers to discriminate against women because of their gender. The 1960s was also a time of technological progress. Britain and France developed the world's only supersonic commercial airliner, Concorde. New styles of architecture, including high-rise buildings and the use of concrete and steel, became common. The number of people migrating from the West Indies, India, Pakistan and what is now Bangladesh fell in the late 1960s because the government passed new laws to restrict immigration to Britain. Immigrants were required to have a strong connection to Britain through birth or ancestry. Even so, during the early 1970s, Britain admitted 28,000 people of Indian origin who had been forced to leave Uganda.

Some great British inventions of the 20th century

Britain has given the world some wonderful inventions. Examples from the 20th century include:

The television was developed by Scotsman John Logie Baird (1888-1946) in the 1920s. In 1932 he made the first television broadcast between London and Glasgow.

Radar was developed by Scotsman Sir Robert Watson-Watt (1892-1973), who proposed that enemy aircraft could be detected by radio waves. The first successful radar test took place in 1935. Working with radar led Sir Bernard Lovell (1913-2012) to make new discoveries in astronomy.

The radio telescope he built at Jodrell Bank in Cheshire was for many years the biggest in the world and continues to operate today.

A Turing machine is a theoretical mathematical device invented by Alan Turing (1912-54), a British mathematician, in the 1930s. The theory was influential in the development of computer science and the modern-day computer.

The Scottish physician and researcher John Macleod (1876-1935) was the codiscoverer of insulin, used to treat diabetes.

The structure of the DNA molecule was discovered in 1953 through work at British universities in London and Cambridge. This discovery contributed to many scientific advances, particularly in medicine and fighting crime.

Francis Crick (1916-2004), one of those awarded the Nobel Prize for this discovery, was British. The jet engine was developed in Britain in the 1930s by Sir Frank Whittle (1907-96), a British Royal Air Force engineer officer.

Sir Christopher Cockrell (1910-99), a British inventor, invented the hovercraft in the 1950s. Britain and France developed Concorde, the world's only supersonic passenger aircraft. It first flew in 1969 and began carrying passengers in 1976. Concorde was retired from service in 2003. The Harrier jump jet, an aircraft capable of taking off vertically, was also designed and developed in the UK. In the 1960s,

James Goodfellow (1937-) invented the cash-dispensing ATM (automatic teller machine) or 'cashpoint'. The first of these was put into use by Barclays Bank in Enfield, north London in 1967. IVF (in-vitro fertilisation) therapy for the treatment of infertility was pioneered in Britain by physiologist Sir Robert Edwards (1925-) and gynaecologist

Patrick Steptoe (1913-88). The world's first 'test-tube baby' was born in Oldham, Lancashire in 1978. In 1996, two British scientists, Sir Ian Wilmot (1944-) and Keith Campbell (1954-2012), led a team which was the first to succeed in cloning a mammal, Dolly the sheep. This has led to further research into the possible use of cloning to preserve endangered species and for medical purposes.

Sir Peter Mansfield (1933-), a British scientist, is the co-inventor of the MRI (magnetic resonance imaging) scanner. This enables doctors and researchers to obtain exact and non-invasive images of human internal organs and has revolutionised diagnostic medicine.

The inventor of the World Wide Web, Sir Tim Berners-Lee (1955-), is British. Information was successfully transferred via the web for the first time on 25 December 1990.

## Problem in the economy in the 1970s

In the late 1970s, the post-war economic boom came to an end. Prices of goods and raw materials began to rise sharply and the exchange rate between the pound and other currencies was unstable. This caused problems with the 'balance of payments': imports of goods were valued at more than the price paid for exports. Many industries and services were affected by strikes and this caused problems between the trade unions and the government. People began to argue that the unions were too powerful and that their activities were harming the UK.

The 1970s were also a time of serious unrest in Northern Ireland. In 1972, the Northern Ireland Parliament was suspended and Northern Ireland was directly ruled by the UK government. Some 3,000 people lost their lives in the decades after 1969 in the violence of Northern Ireland.

## Mary Peters (1939-)

Born in Manchester, Mary Peters moved to Northern Ireland as a child. She was a talented athlete who won an Olympic gold medal in the pentathlon in 1972. After this, she raised money for local athletics and became the team manager for the women's British Olympic team. She continues to promote sport and tourism in Northern Ireland and was made a Dame of the British Empire in 2000 in recognition of her work.

## Europe and the Common Market

West Germany, France, Belgium, Italy, Luxembourg and the Netherlands formed the European Economic Community (EEC) in 1957. At first the UK did not wish to join the EEC but it eventually did so in 1973. The UK voted to leave the EU in 2016 and eventually left the EU in 2020.

## Conservative government from 1979 to 1997

Margaret Thatcher, Britain's first woman Prime Minister, led the Conservative government from 1979 to 1990. The government made structural changes to the economy through the privatisation of nationalised industries and imposed legal controls on trade union powers. Deregulation saw a great increase in the role of the City of London as an international centre for investments, insurance and other financial services. Traditional industries, such as shipbuilding and coal mining, declined. In 1982, Argentina invaded the Falkland Islands, a British overseas territory in the South Atlantic. A naval taskforce was sent from the UK and military action led to the recovery of the islands. John Major was Prime Minister after Mrs Thatcher, and helped establish the Northern Ireland peace process.

## Margaret Thatcher (1925-2013)

Margaret Thatcher was the daughter of a grocer from Grantham in Lincolnshire. She trained as a chemist and lawyer. She was elected as a Conservative MP in 1959 and became a cabinet minister in 1970 as the Secretary of State for Education and Science. In 1975 she was elected as Leader of the Conservative Party and so became Leader of the Opposition. Following the Conservative victory in the General Election in 1979, Margaret Thatcher became the first woman Prime Minister of the UK. She was the longest-serving Prime Minister of the 20th century, remaining in office until 1990. Margaret Thatcher, the first female Prime Minister of the UK During her premiership, there were a number of important economic reforms within the UK. She worked closely with the United States President, Ronald Reagan, and was one of the first Western leaders to recognise and welcome the changes in the leadership of the Soviet Union which eventually led to the end of the Cold War.

## Roald Dahl (1916-90)

Roald Dahl was born in Wales to Norwegian parents. He served in the Royal Air Force during the Second World War. It was during the 1940s that he began to publish books and short stories. He is most well known for his children's books, although he also wrote for adults. His best-known works include Charlie and the Chocolate Factory and George's Marvellous Medicine. Several of his books have been made into films.

## Labour government from 1997 to 2010

In 1997 the Labour Party led by Tony Blair was elected. The Blair government introduced a Scottish Parliament and a Welsh Assembly (see page 129). The Scottish Parliament has substantial powers to legislate. The Welsh Assembly was given fewer legislative powers but considerable control over public services. In Northern Ireland, the Blair government was able to build on the Peace process, resulting in the Good Friday Agreement signed in 1998. The Northern Ireland Assembly was elected in 1999 but suspended in 2002. It was not reinstated until 2007. Most paramilitary groups in Northern Ireland have decommissioned their arms and are inactive. Gordon Brown took over as Prime Minister in 2007.

## Conflicts in Afghanistan and Iraq

Throughout the 1990s, Britain played a leading role in coalition forces involved in the liberation of Kuwait, following the Iraqi invasion in 1990, and the conflict in the former Republic of Yugoslavia. Since 2000, British armed forces have been engaged in the global fight against international terrorism and against the proliferation of weapons of mass destruction, including operations in Afghanistan and Iraq. British combat troops left Iraq in 2009. The UK now operates in Afghanistan as part of the United Nations (UN) mandated 50-nation International Security Assistance Force (ISAF) coalition and at the invitation of the Afghan government. ISAF is working to ensure that Afghan territory can never again be used as a safe haven for international terrorism, where groups such as Al Qa'ida could plan attacks on the international community. As part of this, ISAF is building up the Afghan National Security Forces and is helping to create a secure environment in which governance and development can be extended. International forces are gradually handing over responsibility for security to the Afghans, who will have full security responsibility in all provinces by the end of 2014.

## Coalition government 2010 onwards

In May 2010, and for the first time in the UK since February 1974, no political party won an overall majority in the General Election. The Conservative and Liberal Democrat parties formed a coalition and the leader of the Conservative Party, David Cameron, became Prime Minister.

**Check that you understand**

• **The establishment of the welfare state**
• **How life in Britain changed in the 1960s and 1970s**
• **British inventions of the 20th century (you do not need to remember dates of births and deaths)**
• **Events since 1979**

# Chapter 4 - A Modern, Thriving Society

## The UK today

The UK today is a more diverse society than it was 100 years ago, in both ethnic and religious terms. Post-war immigration means that nearly 10% of the population has a parent or grandparent born outside the UK. The UK continues to be a multinational and multiracial society with a rich and varied culture. This section will tell you about the different parts of the UK and some of the important places. It will also explain some of the UK's traditions and customs and some of the popular activities that take place. The nations of the UK The UK is located in the north west of Europe. The longest distance on the mainland is from John O'Groats on the north coast of Scotland to Land's End in the south-west corner of England. It is about 870 miles (approximately 1,400 kilometres).

Most people live in towns and cities but much of Britain is still countryside. Many people continue to visit the countryside for holidays and for leisure activities such as walking, camping and fishing.

## Languages and dialects

There are many variations in language in the different parts of the UK. The English language has many accents and dialects. In Wales, many people speak Welsh – a completely different language from English – and it is taught in schools and universities. In Scotland, Gaelic (again, a different language) is spoken in some parts of the Highlands and Islands, and in Northern Ireland some people speak Irish Gaelic.

## Population

Population growth has been faster in more recent years. Migration into the UK and longer life expectancy have played a part in population growth. The population is very unequally distributed over the four parts of the UK. England more or less consistently makes up 84% of the total population, Wales around 5%, Scotland just over 8%, and Northern Ireland less than 3%.

### An ageing population

People in the UK are living longer than ever before. This is due to improved living standards and better health care. There are now a record number of people aged 85 and over. This has an impact on the cost of pensions and health care.

# Ethnic diversity

The UK population is ethnically diverse and changing rapidly, especially in large cities such as London. It is not always easy to get an exact picture of the ethnic origin of all the population. There are people in the UK with ethnic origins from all over the world. In surveys, the most common ethnic description chosen is white, which includes people of European, Australian, Canadian, New Zealand and American descent. Other significant groups are those of Asian, black and mixed descent.

# An Equal Society

Within the UK, it is a legal requirement that men and women should not be discriminated against because of their gender or because the are, or are not, married. They have equal rights to work, own property, marry and divorce. If they are married, both parents are equally responsible for their children.

Women in Britain today make up about half of the workforce. On average, girls leave school with better qualifications than boys. More women than men study at university. Employment opportunities for women are much greater than they were in the past. Women work in all sectors of the economy, and there are now more women in high-level positions than ever before, including senior mangers in traditionally male-dominated occupations. Alongside this, men now work in more varied jobs than they did in the past. It is no longer expected that women should stay at home and not work. Women often continue to work after having children. In many families today, both partners work and both share responsibility for childcare and household chores.

**Check that you understand**

- **The capital cites of the UK**
- **What languages other than English are spoken in particular parts of the UK**
- **How the population of the UK has changed**
- **That the UK is and equal society and ethnically diverse**
- **The currency of the UK**

# Religion

The UK is historically a Christian country. In the 2009 Citizenship Survey, 70% of people identified themselves as Christian. Much smaller proportions identified themselves as Muslim (4%), Hindu (2%), Sikh (1%), Jewish or Buddhist (both less than 0.5%), and 2% of people followed another religion. There are religious buildings for other religions all over the UK. This includes Islamic mosques, Hindu temples, Jewish synagogues, Sikh gurdwaras and Buddhist temples. However, everyone has the legal right to choose their religion, or to choose not to practice a religion. In the Citizenship Survey, 21% of people said that they had no religion.

# Christian churches

In England, there is a constitutional link between Church and state. The official Church of the state is the Church of England (called the Anglican Church in other countries and the Episcopal Church in Scotland and the United States). It is a Protestant Church and has existed since the Reformation in the 1530s. The monarch is the head of the Church of England. The spiritual leader of the Church of England is the Archbishop of Canterbury. The monarch has the right to select the Archbishop and other senior church officials, but usually the choice is made by the Prime Minister and a committee appointed by the Church. Several Church of England bishops sit in the House of Lords.

In Scotland, the national Church is the Church of Scotland, which is a Presbyterian Church. It is governed by ministers and elders. The chairperson of the General Assembly of the Church of Scotland is the Moderator, who is appointed for one year only and often speaks on behalf of that Church. There is no established Church in Wales or Northern Ireland. Other Protestant Christian groups in the UK are Baptists, Methodists, Presbyterians and Quakers. There are also other denominations of Christianity, the biggest of which is Roman Catholic.

# Patron saints' days

England, Scotland, Wales and Northern Ireland each have a national saint, called a patron saint. Each saint has a special day:

- 1 March: St David's Day, Wales
- 17 March: St Patrick's Day, Northern Ireland
- 23 April: St George's Day, England
- 30 November: St Andrew's Day, Scotland.

Only Scotland and Northern Ireland have their patron saint's day as an official holiday (although in Scotland not all businesses and offices will close). Events are held across Scotland, Northern Ireland and the rest of the country, especially where there are a lot of people of Scottish, Northern Irish and Irish heritage. While the patron saints' days are no longer public holidays in England and Wales, they are still celebrated. Parades and small festivals are held all over the two countries.

**Check that you understand**

- **The different religions that are practised in the UK**

- **That the Anglican Church, also known as the Church of England, is the Church of the state in England (the 'established Church')**

- **That other branches of the Christian Church also practise their faith in the UK without being linked to the state**

- **That other religions are practised in the UK**

- **About the patron saints**

# Customs and traditions

**Christmas Day, 25 December**, celebrates the birth of Jesus Christ. It is a public holiday. Many Christians go to church on Christmas Eve (24 December) or on Christmas Day itself. Christmas is celebrated in a traditional way. People usually spend the day at home and eat a special meal, which often includes roast turkey, Christmas pudding and mince pies. They give gifts, send cards and decorate their houses. Christmas is a special time for children. Very young children believe that Father Christmas (also known as Santa Claus) brings them presents during the night before Christmas Day. Many people decorate a tree in their home.

**Boxing Day** is the day after Christmas Day and is a public holiday.

**Easter** takes place in March or April. It marks the death of Jesus Christ on Good Friday and his rising from the dead on Easter Sunday. Both Good Friday and the following Monday, called Easter Monday, are public holidays. The 40 days before Easter are known as Lent. It is a time when Christians take time to reflect and prepare for Easter. Traditionally, people would fast during this period and today many people will give something up, like a favourite food. The day before Lent starts is called Shrove Tuesday, or Pancake Day. People eat pancakes, which were traditionally made to use up foods such as eggs, fat and milk before fasting. Lent begins on Ash Wednesday. There are church services where Christians are marked with an ash cross on their forehead as a symbol of death and sorrow for sin. Easter is also celebrated by people who are not religious. 'Easter eggs' are chocolate eggs given as presents as a symbol of new life.

# Other religious festivals

**Diwali** normally falls in October or November and lasts for five days. It is often called the Festival of Lights. It is celebrated by Hindus and Sikhs. It celebrates the victory of good over evil and the gaining of knowledge. There are different stories about how the festival came about. There is a famous celebration of Diwali in Leicester.

**Hannukah** is in November or December and is celebrated for eight days. It is to remember the Jews' struggle for religious freedom. On each day of the festival a candle is lit on a stand of eight candles (called a menorah) to remember the story of the festival, where oil that should have lasted only a day did so for eight.

**Eid a-Fitr** celebrates the end of Ramadan, when Muslims have fasted for a month. They thank Allah for giving them the strength to complete the fast. The date when it takes place changes every year. Muslims attend special services and meals.

**Eid ul Adha** remembers that the prophet Ibrahim was willing to sacrifice his son when God ordered him to . It reminds Muslims of their own commitment to God. Many Muslims sacrifice an animal to eat during this festival. In Britain this has to be done in a slaughterhouse.

**Vaisakhi** (also spelled Baisakhi) is a Sikh festival which celebrates the founding of the Sikh community known as the Khalsa. It is celebrated on 14 April each year with parades, dancing and singing.

## Other festivals and traditions

**New Year**, 1 January, is a public holiday. People usually celebrate on the night of 31 December (called New Year's Eve). In Scotland, 31 December is called Hogmanay and 2 January is also a public holiday. For some Scottish people, Hogmanay is a bigger holiday than Christmas.

**Valentine's Day**, 14 February, is when lovers exchange cards and gifts. Sometimes people send anonymous cards to someone they secretly admire.

**April Fool's Day**, 1 April, is a day when people play jokes on each other until midday. The television and newspapers often have stories that are April Fool jokes.

**Mothering Sunday** (or Mother's day) is the Sunday three weeks before Easter. Children send cards or buy gifts for their mothers.

**Father's Day** is the third Sunday in June. Children send cards or buy gifts for their fathers.

**Halloween,** 31 October, is an ancient festival and has roots in the pagan festival to mark the beginning of winter. Young people will often dress up in frightening costumes to play 'trick or treat'. People give them treats to stop them playing tricks on them. A lot of people carve lanterns out of pumpkins and put a candle inside of them.

**Bonfire Night**, 5 November, is an occasion when people in Great Britain set off fireworks at home or in special displays. The origin of this celebration was an event in 1605, when a group of Catholics led by Guy Fawkes failed in their plan to kill the Protestant king with a bomb in the Houses of Parliament.

**Remembrance Day**, 11 November, commemorates those who died fighting for the UK and its allies. Originally it commemorated the dead of the First World War, which ended on 11 November 1918. People wear poppies (the red flower found on the battlefields of the First World War). At 11.00 am there is a two-minute silence and wreaths are laid at the Cenotaph in Whitehall, London.

## Bank Holidays

As well as those mentioned previously, there are other public holidays each year called bank holidays, when banks and many other businesses are closed for the day. These are of no religious significance. They are at the beginning of May in late May or early June, and in August. In Northern Ireland, the anniversary of the Battle of the Boyne in July is also a public holiday.

**Check that you understand**

• **The main Christian festivals that are celebrated in the UK**
• **Other religious festivals that are important in the UK**
• **Some of the other events that are celebrated in the UK**

## Sport

Sports of all kinds play an important part in many people's lives. There are several sports that are particularly popular in the UK. Many sporting events take place at major stadiums such as Wembley Stadium in London and the Millennium Stadium in Cardiff. Local governments and private companies provide sports facilities such as swimming pools, tennis courts, football pitches, dry ski slopes and gymnasiums. Many famous sports, including cricket, football, lawn tennis, golf and rugby, began in Britain. The UK has hosted the Olympic games on three occasions: 1908, 1948 and 2012. The main Olympic site for the 2012 Games was in Stratford, East London.

The British team was very successful, across a wide range of Olympic sports, finishing third in the medal table. The Paralympic Games for 2012 were also hosted in London. The Paralympics have their origin in the work of Dr Sir Ludwig Guttman, a German refugee, at the Stoke Mandeville hospital in Buckinghamshire. Dr Guttman developed new methods of treatment for people with spinal injuries and encouraged patients to take part in exercise and sport.

## Notable British sportsmen and women

Sir Roger Bannister (1929-) was the first man in the world to run a mile in under four minutes, in 1954.

Sir Jackie Stewart (1939-) is a Scottish former racing driver who won the Formula 1 world championship three times.

Bobby Moore (1941-93) captained the English football team that won the World Cup in 1966.

Sir Ian Botham (1955-) captained the English cricket team and holds a number of English Test cricket records, both for batting and for bowling.

Jayne Torvill (1957_) and Christopher Dean (1958-) won gold medals for ice dancing at the Olympic Games in 1984 and are some of Britain's greatest Olympians.

Sir Steve Redgrave (1962-) won gold medals in rowing in five consecutive Olympic Games and is one of Britain's greatest Olympians.

Baroness Tanni Grey-Thompson (1969-) is an athlete who uses a wheelchair and won 16 Paralympic medals, including 11 gold medals, in races over five Paralympic Games. She won the London Marathon six times and broke a total of 30 world records.

Dame Kelly Holmes (1970_) won two gold medals for running in the 2004 Olympic Games. She has held a number of British and European records.

Dame Ellen MacArthur (1976-) is a yachtswoman and in 2004 became the fastest person to sail around the world singlehanded.

Sir Chris Hoy (1976-) is a Scottish cyclist who has won six gold and one silver Olympic medals. He has also won 11 world championship titles.

David Weir (1979-) is a Paralympian who uses a wheelchair and has won six gold medals over two Paralympic Games. He has also won the London Marathon six times.

Bradley Wiggins (1980-) is a cyclist. In 2012, he became the first Briton to win the Tour de France. He has won seven Olympic Medals, including gold medals in the 2004, 2008 and 2012 Olympic Games.

Mo Farah (1983-) is a British distance runner, born in Somalia. He won gold medals in the 2012 Olympics for the 5,000 and 10,000 metres and is the first Briton to win the Olympic gold medal in the 10,000 metres.

Jessica Ennis (1986-) is an athlete. She won the 2012 Olympic gold medal in the heptathlon, which includes seven different track and field events. She also holds a number of British athletics records.

Andy Murray (1987-) is a Scottish tennis player who in 2012 won the men's singles in the US Open. He is the first British man to win a singles title in a Grand Slam tournament since 1936.

Ellie Simmonds (1994-) is a Paralympian who won gold medals for swimming at the 2008 and 2012 Paralympic Games and holds a number of world records. She was the youngest member of the British team at the 2008 Games.

## Cricket

Cricket originated in England and is now played in many countries. Games can last up to five days but still result in a draw! The idiosyncratic nature of the game and its complex laws are said to reflect the best of the British character and sense of fair play. You may come across expressions such as 'rain stopped play', 'batting on a sticky wicket', 'playing a straight bat', 'bowled a googly' or 'it's just not cricket', which have passed into everyday usage. The most famous competition is the Ashes, which is a series of Test matches played between England and Australia.

## Football

Football is the UK's most popular sport. It has a long history in the UK and the first professional football clubs were formed in the late 19th century. England, Scotland, Wales and Northern Ireland each have separate leagues in which clubs representing different towns and cities compete. The English Premier League attracts a huge international audience. Many UK teams also compete in competitions such as the UEFA (Union of European Football Associations) Champions League, against other teams from Europe. Most towns and cities have a professional club and people take great pride in supporting their home team. There can be great pride in supporting their home team.

There can be great rivalry between different football clubs and among fans. Each country in the UK also has its own national team that competes with other national teams across the world in tournaments such as the FIFA (Fédération Internationale de Football Association) World Cup and UEFA

European Football Championships. England's only international tournament victory was at the World Cup of 1966, hosted in the UK. Football is also a popular sport to play in many local communities, with people playing amateur games every week in parks all over the UK.

## Rugby

Rugby originated in England in the early 19th century and is very popular in the UK today. There are two different types of rugby, which have different rules: union and league. Both have separate leagues and national teams in England , Wales, Scotland and Northern Ireland (who play with the Irish Republic). Teams from all countries compete in a range of competitions. The most famous rugby union competition is the Six Nations Championship between England, Ireland, Scotland, Wales, France and Italy. The Super League is the most well-known rugby league (club) competition.

## Horse Racing

There is a very long history of horse racing in Britain, with evidence of events taking place as far back as Roman times. The sport has a long association with royalty. There are racecourses all over the UK. Famous horse-racing events include: Royal Ascot , a five-day race meeting in Berkshire attended by members of the Royal Family; the Grand National at Aintree near Liverpool; and the Scottish Grand National at Ayr. There is a National Horseracing Museum in Newmarket, Suffolk.

## Golf

The modern game of golf can be traced back to 15th century Scotland. It is a popular sport played socially as well as professionally. There are public and private golf courses all over the UK. St Andrews in Scotland is known as the home of golf. The open championship is the only 'Major' tournament held outside the United States. It is hosted by a different golf course every year.

## Tennis

Modern tennis evolved in England in the late 19th century. The first tennis club was founded in Leamington Spa in 1872. The most famous tournament hosted in Britain is The Wimbledon Championships, which takes place each year at the All England Lawn Tennis and Croquet Club. It is the oldest tennis tournament in the world and the only 'Grand Slam' event played on grass.

## Water Sports

Sailing continues to be popular in the UK, reflecting our maritime heritage. A British sailor, Sir Francis Chichester, was the first person to sail singlehanded around the world, in 1966/67. Two years later, Sir Robin KnoxJohnston became the first person to do this without stopping. Many sailing events are held throughout the UK, the most famous of which is at Cowes on the Isle of

Wight. Rowing is also popular, both as a leisure activity and as a competitive sport. There is a popular yearly race on the Thames between Oxford and Cambridge Universities.

## Motor sports

There is a long history of motor sport in the UK, for both cars and motor cycles. Motor-car racing in the UK started in 1902. The UK continues to be a world leader in the development and manufacture of motor-sport technology. A Formula 1 Grand Prix event is held in the UK each year and a number of British Grand Prix drivers have won the Formula 1 World Championship. Recent British winners include Damon Hill, Lewis Hamilton and Jenson Button.

## Skiing

Skiing is increasingly popular in the UK. Many people go abroad to ski and there are also dry slopes throughout the UK. Skiing on snow may also be possible during the winter. There are five ski centres in Scotland, as well as Europe's longest dry ski slope near Edinburgh.

## Arts and culture

Music is an important part of British culture, with a rich and varied heritage. It ranges from classical music to modern pop. There are many different venues and musical events that take place across the UK. The Proms is an eight-week summer season of orchestral classical music that takes place in various venues, including the Royal Albert Hall in London. It has been in various venues, including the Royal Albert Hall in London. It has been organised by the British Broadcasting Corporation (BBC) since 1927.

The Last Night of the Proms is the most well-known concert and (along with others in the series) is broadcast on television.

Classical music has been popular in the UK for centuries. **Henry Purcell (1659-95)** was the organist at Westminster Abbey. He wrote church music, operas and other pieces, and developed a British style distinct from that elsewhere in Europe. He continues to be influential on British composers.

The German-born composer **George Frederick Handel (1685-1759)** spent many years in the UK and became a British citizen in 1727. He wrote the Water Music for King George I and Music for the Royal Fireworks for his son, George II. Both these pieces continue to be very popular. Handel also wrote an oratorio, Messiah, which is sung regularly by choirs, often at Easter time.

More recently, important composers include **Gustav Holst (1874-1934)**, whose work includes The Planets, a suite of pieces themed around the planets and the solar system. He adapted Jupiter, part of the Planets suite, as the tune for I owe to thee my country, a popular hymn in British churches.

**Sir Edward Elgar (1857-1934)** was born in Worcester, England. His bestknown work is probably the Pomp and Circumstance Marches. March No1 (Land of Hope and Glory) is usually played at the Last Night of the Proms at the Royal Albert Hall.

**Ralph Vaughan Williams (1872-1958)** wrote music for orchestras and choirs. He was strongly influenced by traditional English folk music.

**Sir William Walton (1902-83)** wrote a wide range of music, from film scores to opera. He wrote marches for the coronations of King George VI and Queen Elizabeth II but his best-known works are probably Façade, which became a ballet, and Balthazar's Feast, which is intended to be sung by a large choir.

Benjamin Britten (1913-76) is best known for his operas, which include Peter Grimes and Billy Budd. He also wrote A Young Person's Guide to the Orchestra, which is based on a piece of music by Purcell and introduces the listener to the various different sections of an orchestra. He founded the Aldeburgh festival in Suffolk, which continues to be a popular music event of international importance.

Other types of popular music, including folk music, jazz, pop and rock music, have flourished in Britain since the 20th century. Britain has had an impact on popular music around the world, due to the wide use of the English language, the UK's cultural links with many countries, and British capacity for invention and innovation. Since the 1960s, British pop music has made one of the most important cultural contributions to life in the UK. Bands including The Beatles and The Rolling Stones continue to have an influence on music both here and abroad. British pop music has continued to innovate – for example, the Punk movement of the late 1970s, and the trend towards boy and girl bands in the 1990s.

There are many large venues that host music events throughout the year, such as: Wembley Stadium; The O2 in Greenwich, south-east London; and the Scottish Exhibition and Conference Centre (SECC) in Glasgow. Festival season takes place across the UK every summer, with major events in various locations. Famous festivals include Glastonbury, the Isle of Wight Festival and the V Festival. Many bands and solo artists, both well-known and up-and-coming, perform at these events.

The National Eisteddfod of Wales is an annual cultural festival which includes music, dance, art and original performances largely in Welsh. It includes a number of important competitions for Welsh poetry.

The Mercury Music Prize is awarded each September for the best album from the UK and Ireland. The Brit Awards is an annual event that gives awards in a range of categories, such as best British group and best British solo artist.

# Theatre

There are theatres in most towns and cities throughout the UK, ranging from the large to the small. They are an important part of local communities and often show both professional and amateur productions. London's west end, also known as 'Theatreland', is particularly well known. The Mousetrap, a murder-mystery play by Dame Agatha Christie, has been running in the west end since 1952 and has had the longest initial run of any show in history. There is also a strong tradition of musical theatre in the UK.

In the 19th century, Gilbert and Sullivan wrote comic operas, often making fun of popular culture and politics. These operas include HMS Pinafore, The Pirates of Penzance and The Mikado. Gilbert and Sullivan's work is still often staged by professional and amateur groups. More recently, Andrew Lloyd Webber has written the music for shows which have been popular throughout the world, including, in collaboration with Tim Rice, Jesus Christ Superstar and Evita, and also Cats and The Phantom of the Opera.

One British tradition is the pantomime. Many theatres produce a pantomime at Christmas time. They are based on fairy stories and are light-hearted plays with music and comedy, enjoyed by family audiences. One of the traditional characters is the Dame, a woman played by a man. There is often also a pantomime horse or cow played by two actors in the same costume. The Edinburgh Festival takes place in Edinburgh, Scotland, every summer. It is a series of different arts and cultural festivals, with the biggest and most well-known being the Edinburgh Festival Fringe ('the Fringe'). The Fringe is a showcase of mainly theatre and comedy performances. It often shows experimental work.

The Laurence Olivier Awards take place annually at different venues in London. There are a variety of categories, including best director, best actor and best actress. The awards are named after the British actor Sir Laurence Olivier, late Lord Olivier, who was best known for his roles in various Shakespeare plays.

# Art

During the Middle Ages, most art had a religious theme, particularly wall paintings in churches and illustrations in religious books. Much of this was lost after the Protestant Reformation but wealthy families began to collect other paintings and sculptures. Many of the painters working in Britain in the 16th and 17th centuries were from abroad-for example, Hans Holbein and Sir Anthony Van Dyck. British artists, particularly those painting portraits and landscapes, became well known from the 18th century onwards. Works by British and international artists are displayed in Galleries across the UK.

Some of the most well-known galleries are The National Gallery, Tate Britain and Tate Modern in London, the National Museum in Cardiff, and the National Gallery of Scotland in Edinburgh.

# Notable British artists

**Thomas Gainsborough (1727-88)** was a portrait painter who often painted people in country or garden scenery.

**David Allan (1744-96)** was a Scottish painter who was best known for painting portraits. One of his most famous works is called The Origin of Painting.

**Joseph Turner (1775-1851)** was an influential landscape painter in a modern style. He is considered the artist who raised the profile of landscape painting.

**John Constable (1776-1837)** was a landscape painter most famous for his works of Dedham Vale on the Suffolk-Essex border in the east of England.

**The Pre-Raphaelites** were an important group of artists in the second half of the 19th century. They painted detailed pictures on religious or literary themes in bright colours. The group included Holman Hunt, Dante Gabriel Rossetti and Sir John Millais.

**Sir John Lavery (1856-1941)** was a very successful Northern Irish portrait painter. His work included painting the Royal Family.

**Henry Moore (1898-1986)** was an English sculptor and artist. He is best known for his large bronze abstract sculptures.

**John Petts (1914-91)** was a Welsh artist, best known for his engravings and stained glass.

**Lucian Freud (1922-2011)** was a German-born British artist. He is best known for his portraits.

**David Hockney (1937-)** was an important contributor to the 'pop art' movement of the 1960s and continues to be influential today.

The Turner Prize was established in 1984 and celebrates contemporary art. It was named after Joseph Turner. Four works are shortlisted every year and shown at Tate Britain before the winner is announced. The Turner Prize is recognised as one of the most prestigious visual art awards in Europe. Previous winners include Damien Hirst and Richard Wright.

## Architecture

The architectural heritage of the UK is rich and varied. In the Middle Ages, great cathedrals and churches were built, many of which still stand today. Examples are the cathedrals in Durham, Lincoln, Canterbury and Salisbury.

The White Tower in the Tower of London is an example of a Norman castle keep, built on the orders of William the Conqueror. Gradually, as the countryside became more peaceful and landowners became richer, the houses of the wealthy became more elaborate and great country houses such as Hardwick Hall in Derbyshire were built. British styles of architecture began to evolve. In the 17th century, Inigo Jones took inspiration from classical architecture to design the Queen's House at Greenwich and the Banqueting House in Whitehall in London.

Later in the century, Sir Christopher Wren helped develop a British version of the ornate styles popular in Europe in buildings such as the new St Paul's Cathedral. In the 18th century, simpler designs became popular. The Scottish architect Robert Adam influenced the development of architecture in the UK, Europe and America. He designed the inside decoration as well as the building itself in great houses such as Dumfries House in Scotland. His ideas influenced architects in cities such as Bath, where the Royal Crescent was built. In the 19th century, the medieval 'gothic' style became popular again. As cities expanded, many great public buildings were built in this style. The Houses of Parliament and St Pancras Station were built at this time, as were the town halls in cities such as Manchester and Sheffield. In the 20th century, Sir Edwin Lutyens had an influence throughout the British Empire. He designed New Delhi to be the seat of government in India. After the First World War, he was responsible for many war memorials throughout the world, including the Cenotaph in Whitehall. The Cenotaph is the site of the annual Remembrance Day service attended by the Queen, politicians and foreign ambassadors.

Modern British architects including Sir Norman Foster and Lord (Richard) Rogers continue to work on major projects throughout the world as well as within the UK.

Alongside the development of architecture, garden design and landscaping have played an important role in the UK. In the 18th century, Lancelot 'Capability' Brown designed the grounds around country houses so that the landscape appeared to be natural, with grass, trees and lakes. He often said that a place had 'capabilities'. Later, Gertrude Jekyll often worked with worked with Edwin Lutyens to design colourful gardens around the houses he designed. Gardens continue to be an important part of homes in the UK. The annual Chelsea Flower Show showcases garden design from Britain and around the world.

# Fashion and design

Britain has produced many great designers, from Thomas Chippendale (who designed furniture in the 18th century) to Clarice Cliff (who designed Art Deco ceramics) to Sir Terence Conran (a 20th-century interior designer). Leading fashion designers of recent years include Mary Quant, Alexander McQueen and Vivienne Westwood.

# Literature

The UK has a prestigious literary history and tradition. Several British writers, including the novelist Sir William Golding, the poet Seamus Heaney, and the playwright Harold Pinter, have won the Nobel Prize in Literature. Other authors have become well known in popular fiction. Agatha Christie's detective stories are read all over the world and Ian Fleming's books introduced James Bond. In 2003, The Lord of the Rings by JRR Tolkien was voted the country's best-loved novel. The Man Booker Prize for Fiction is awarded annually for the best fiction novel written by an author from the Commonwealth, Ireland or Zimbabwe. It has been awarded since 1968. Past winners include Ian McEwan, Hilary Mantel and Julian Barnes.

## Notable authors and writers

**Jane Austen (1775-1817)** was an English novelist. Her books include Pride and Prejudice and Sense and Sensibility. Her novels are concerned with marriage and family relationships. Many have been made into television programmes or films.

**Charles Dickens (1812-70)** wrote a number of very famous novels, including Oliver twist and Great Expectations. You will hear references in everyday talk to some of the characters in his books, such as Scrooge (a mean person) or Mr Micawber (always hopeful).

**Robert Louis Stevenson (1850-94)** wrote books which are still read by adults and children today. His most famous books include Treasure Island, Kidnapped and Dr Jekyll and Mr Hyde.

**Thomas Hardy (1840-1928)** was an author and poet. His best-known novels focus on rural society and include Far from the Madding Crowd and Jude the Obscure.

**Sir Arthur Conan Doyle (1859-1930)** was a Scottish doctor and writer. He was best known for his stories about Sherlock Holmes, who was one of the first fictional detectives.

**Evelyn Waugh (1903-66)** wrote satirical novels, including Decline and Fall and Scoop. He is perhaps best known for Brideshead Revisited.

**Sir Kingsley Amis (1922-95)** was an English novelist and poet. He wrote more than 20 novels. The most well known is Lucky Jim.

**Graham Greene (1904-91)** wrote novels often influenced by his religious beliefs, including The Heart of the Matter, The Honorary Consul, Brighton Rock and Our Man in Havana. J K Rowling (1965-) wrote the Harry Potter series of children's books, which have enjoyed huge international success. She now writes fiction for adults as well.

# British Poets

British poetry is among the richest in the world. The Anglo-Saxon poem Beowulf tells of its hero's battles against monsters and is still translated into modern English. Poems which survive from the Middle Ages include Chaucer's Canterbury Tales and a poem called Sir Gawain and the Green Knight, about one of the knights at the court of King Arthur.

As well as plays, Shakespeare wrote many sonnets (poems which must be 14 lines long) and some longer poems. As Protestant ideas spread, a number of poets wrote poems inspired by their religious views. One of these was John Milton, who wrote Paradise Lost.

Other poets, including William Wordsworth, were inspired by nature. Sir Walter Scott wrote poems inspired by Scotland and the traditional stories and songs from the area on the borders of Scotland and England. He also wrote novels, many of which were set in Scotland. Poetry was very popular in the 19th century, with poets such as William Blake, John Keats, Lord Byron, Percy Shelley, Alfred Lord Tennyson, and Robert and Elizabeth Browning.

Later, many poets-for example, Wilfred Owen and Siegfried Sassoon – were inspired to write about their experiences in the First World War. More recently, popular poets have included Sir Walter de la Mare, John Masefield, Sir John Betjeman and Ted Hughes. Some of the best-known poets are buried or commemorated in Poet's Corner in Westminster Abbey.

Some famous lines include:

'Oh, to be in England now that April's there And whoever wakes in England sees, some morning, unaware, That the lowest boughs and the brushwood sheaf Round the elm-tree bole are in tiny leaf While the Chaffinch sings on the orchard bough In England – Now!' (Robert Browning, 1812-89 – Home Thoughts from Abroad)

'She walks in beauty, like the night Of cloudless climes and starry skies, All that's best of dark and bright Meet in her aspect and her eyes' (Lord Byron, 1788-1824 – She walks in Beauty)

'I wander'd lonely as a cloud That floats on high o'er vales and hills When all at once I saw a crowd, A host of golden daffodils' (William Wordsworth, 1770-1850 – The Daffodils)

'Tyger! Tyger! Burning bright In the forests of the night, What immortal hand and eye Could frame thy fearful symmetry?' (William Blake, 1757-1827 – The Tyger)

'What passing-bells for these who die as cattle? Only the monstrous anger of the guns. Only the stuttering rifles' rapid rattle Can patter out their hasty orisons.' (Wilfred Owen, 1893-1918 – Anthem for Doomed Youth)

**Check that you understand**

• **Which sports are particularly popular in the UK**
• **Some of the major sporting events that take place each year**

# Leisure

People in the UK spend their leisure time in many different ways.

# Gardening

A lot of people have gardens at home and will spend their free time looking after them. Some people rent additional land called 'an allotment', where they grow fruit and vegetables. Gardening and flower shows range from major national exhibitions to small local events. Many towns have garden centres selling plants and gardening equipment. There are famous gardens to visit throughout the UK, including Kew Gardens, Sissinghurst and Hidcote in England, Crathes Castle and Inveraray Castle in Scotland, Bodnant Garden in Wales, and Mount Stewart in Northern Ireland.

The countries that make up the UK all have flowers which are particularly associated with them and which are sometimes worn on national saints' days:

• England – the rose
• Scotland – the thistle
• Wales – the daffodil
• Northern Ireland – the shamrock.

# Shopping

There are many different places to go shopping in the UK. Most towns and cities have a central shopping area, which is called the town centre. Undercover shopping centres are also common – these might be in town centres or on the outskirts of a town or city. Most shops in the UK are open seven days a week, although trading hours on Sundays and public holidays are generally reduced. Many towns also have markets on one or more days a week, where stallholders sell a variety of goods.

# Cooking and food

Many people in the UK enjoy cooking. They often invite each other to their homes for dinner. A wide variety of food is eaten in the UK because of the country's rich cultural heritage and diverse population.

# Traditional foods

There are a variety of foods that are traditionally associated with different parts of the UK:

• England: Roast beef, which is served with potatoes, vegetables, Yorkshire puddings (batter that is baked in the oven) and other accompaniments. Fish and chips are also popular.

• Wales: welsh cakes – traditional Welsh snack made from flour, dried fruits and spices, and served either hot or cold.

• Scotland: Haggis – a sheep's stomach stuffed with offal. Suet, onions and oatmeal.

• Northern Ireland: Ulster fry – a fried meal with bacon, eggs, sausage, black pudding, tomatoes, mushrooms, soda bread and potato bread.

# British film industry

The UK has had a major influence on modern cinema. Films were first shown publicly in the UK in 1896 and film screenings very quickly became popular. From the beginning, British film makers became famous for clever special effects and this continues to be an area of British expertise. From the early days of the cinema, British actors have worked in both UK and USA. Sir Charles (Charlie) Chaplin became famous in silent movies for his tramp character and was one of many British actors to make a career in Hollywood. British studios flourished in the 1930s.

Eminent directors included Sir Alexander Korda and Sir Alfred Hitchcock, who later left for Hollywood and remained an important film director until his death in 1980. During the Second World War, British movies (for example, In Which We Serve) played an important part in boosting morale. Later, British directors including Sir David Lean and Ridley Scott found great success both in the UK and internationally. The 1950s and 1960s were a high point for British comedies, including Passport to Pimlico, The Ladykilllers and, later, the Carry On Films.

Many of the films now produced in the UK are made by foreign companies, using British expertise. Some of the most commercially successful films of all time, including the two highest-grossing film franchises (Harry Potter and James Bond), have been produced in the UK. Ealing Studios has a claim to being the oldest continuously working film studio facility in the world. Britain continues to be particularly strong in special effects and animation. One example is the work of Nick Park, who has won four Oscars for his animated films, including three for films featuring Wallace and Gromit.

Actors such as Sir Lawrence Olivier, David Niven, Sir Rex Harrison and Richard Burton starred in a wide variety of popular films. British actors continue to be popular and continue to win awards throughout the world. Recent British actors to have won Oscars include Colin Firth, Sir Antony Hopkins, Dame Judi Dench, Kate Winslet and Tilda Swinton. The annual British Academy Film Awards, hosted by the British Academy of Film and Television Arts (BAFTA), are the British equivalent of the Oscars.

**Some famous British films**

• The 39 Steps (1935), directed by Alfred Hitchcock
• Brief Encounter (1945), directed by David Lean
• The Third Man (1949), directed by Carol Reed
• The Belles of St Trinian's (1954), directed by Frank Launder
• Lawrence of Arabia (1962), directed by David Lean
• Women in Love (1969), directed by Ken Russel
• Don't Look Now (1973), directed by Nicolas Roeg
• Chariots of Fire (1981), directed by Hugh Hudson
• The Killing Fields (1984), directed by Roland Joffé
• Four Weddings and a Funeral (1994), directed by Mike Newell
• Touching the Void (2003), directed by Kevin MacDonald

# British comedy

The traditions of comedy and satire, and the ability to laugh at ourselves, are an important part of the UK character. Medieval kings and rich nobles had jesters who told jokes and made fun of people in the Court. Later, Shakespeare included comic characters in his plays. In the 18th century, political cartoons attacking prominent politicians – and, sometimes, the monarch or other members of the Royal Family – became increasingly popular. In the 19th century, satirical magazines began to be published. The most famous was Punch, which was published for the first time in the 1840s.

Today, political cartoons continue to be published in newspapers, and magazines such as Private Eye continue the tradition of satire. Comedians were a popular feature of British music hall, a form of variety theatre which was very common until television became the leading form of entertainment in the UK. Some of the people who had performed in the music halls in the 1940s and 1950s, such as Morecambe and Wise, became stars of television.

Television comedy developed its own style. Situation comedies, or sitcoms, which often look at family life and relationships in the workplace, remain popular. Satire has also continued to be important, with shows like That Was The Week That Was in the 1960s and Spitting Image in the 1980s and 1990s. In 1969, Monty Python's Flying Circus introduced a new type of progressive comedy. Stand-up comedy, where a solo comedian talks to a live audience, has become popular again in recent years.

# Television and radio

Many different television (TV) channels are available in the UK. Some are free to watch a wide variety of programmes. Popular programmes include regular soap operas such as Coronation Street and EastEnders. In Scotland, some Scotland-specific programmes are shown and there is also a channel with programmes in the Gaelic language.

There is a Welsh-language channel in Wales. There are also programmes specific to Northern Ireland and some programmes broadcast in Irish Gaelic. Everyone in the UK with a TV, computer or other medium which can be used for watching TV must have a television licence. One licence covers all of the equipment in one home, except when people rent different rooms in a shared house and each has a separate tenancy agreement – those people must each buy a separate licence. People over 75 can apply for a free TV licence and blind people can get a 50% discount. You will receive a fine up to £1,000 if you watch TV but do not have a TV licence. The money from TV licences is used to pay for the British Broadcasting Corporation (BBC). This is a public service broadcaster providing television and radio programmes.

The BBC is the largest broadcaster in the world. It is the only wholly state-funded media organisation that is independent of government. Other UK channels are primarily funded through advertisements and subscriptions.

There are also many different radio stations in the UK. Some broadcast nationally and others in certain cities or regions. There are radio stations that play certain types of music and some broadcast in regional languages such as Welsh or Gaelic. Like television, BBC radio stations are funded by TV licences and other radio stations are funded through advertisements.

## Social networking

Social networking websites such as Facebook and Twitter are a popular way for people to stay in touch with friends, organise social events, and share photos, videos and opinions. Many people use social networking on their mobile phones when out and about.

## Pubs and night clubs

Public houses (pubs) are an important part of the UK social culture. Many people enjoy meeting friends in the pub. Most communities will have a 'local' pub that is a natural focal point for social activities. Pub quizzes are popular. Pool and darts are traditional pub games. To buy alcohol in a pub or night club you must be 18 or over, but people under that age may be allowed in some pubs with an adult. When they are 16, people can drink wine or beer with a meal in a hotel or restaurant (including eating areas in pubs) as long as they are with someone over 18. Pubs are usually open during the day from 11.00 am (12 noon on Sundays). Night clubs with dancing and music usually open and close later than pubs. The licensee decides the hours that the pub or night club is open.

## Betting and gambling

In the UK, people often enjoy a gamble on sports or other events. There are also casinos in many places. You have to be 18 to go into betting shops or gambling clubs. There is a National Lottery for which draws are made every week. You can enter by buying a ticket or a scratch card. People under 16 are not allowed to participate in the National Lottery.

## Pets

A lot of people in the UK have pets such as cats or dogs. They might have them for company or because they enjoy looking after them. It is against the law to treat a pet cruelly or to neglect it. All dogs in public places must wear a collar showing the name and address of the owner. The owner is responsible for keeping the dog under control and for cleaning up after the animal in a public place.

Vaccinations and medical treatment for animals are available from veterinary surgeons (vets). There are charities which may help people who cannot afford to pay a vet.

# Places of interest

The UK has a large network of public footpaths in the countryside. There are also many opportunities for mountain biking, mountaineering and hill walking. There are 15 national parks in England, Wales and Scotland. They are areas of protected countryside that everyone can visit, and where people live, work and look after the landscape. There are many museums in the UK, which range from small community museums to large national and civic collections. Famous landmarks exist in towns, cities and the countryside throughout the UK. Most of them are open to the public to view (generally for a charge).

Many parts of the countryside and places of interest are kept open by the National Trust in England, Wales and Northern Ireland and the National Trust for Scotland. Both are charities that work to preserve important buildings, coastline and countryside in the UK. The National Trust was founded in 1895 by three volunteers. There are now more than 61,000 volunteers helping to keep the organisation running.

# UK Landmarks

**Big Ben** is the nickname for the great bell of the clock at the House of Parliament in London. Many people call the clock Big Ben as well. The clock is over 150 years old and is a popular tourist attraction. The clock is named 'Elizabeth Tower' in honour of Queen Elizabeth II's Diamond Jubilee in 2012.

**The Eden Project** is located in Cornwall, in the south west of England. Its biomes, which are like giant greenhouses, house plants from all over the world. The Eden Project is also a charity which runs environmental and social projects internationally.

Edinburgh Castle - The castle is a dominant feature of the skyline in Edinburgh, Scotland. It has a long history, dating back to the early Middle Ages. It is looked after by Historic Scotland, a Scottish government agency.

Located on the north-east coast of Northern Ireland, the Giant's Causeway is a land formation of columns made from volcanic lava. It was formed about 50 million years ago. There are many legends about the Causeway and how it was formed.

Loch Lomond and the Trossachs National Park. This national park covers 720 square miles (1,865 square kilometres) in the west of Scotland. Loch Lomond is the largest expanse of fresh water in mainland Britain and probably the best-known part of the park.

The London Eye is situated on the southern bank of the River Thames and is a Ferris wheel that is 443 feet (135 metres) tall. It was originally built as part of the UK's celebration of the new millennium and continues to be an important part of New Year celebrations.

Snowdonia is a national park in North Wales. It covers an area of 838 square miles (2,170 square kilometres). Its most well-known landmark is Snowdon, which is the highest mountain in Wales.

The Tower of London was first built by William the Conqueror after he became king in 1066. Tours are given by the Yeoman Warders, also known as Beefeaters, who tell visitors about the building's history. People can also see the Crown Jewels there.

The Lake District is England's largest national park. It covers 885 square miles (2,292 square kilometres). It is famous for its lakes and mountains and is very popular with climbers, walkers and sailors. The biggest stretch of water is Windermere. In 2007, television viewers voted Wastwater as Britain's favourite view.

**Check that you understand**

- **Some of the ways in which people in the UK spend their leisure time**
- **The development of British cinema**
- **What the television licence is and how it funds the BBC**
- **Some of the places of interest to visit in the UK**

# Chapter 5 - The UK Government, the Law and Your Role

Chapter contents

• The development of British democracy
• The British constitution
• The government
• The UK and international institutions
• Respecting the law
• Fundamental principles
• Your role in the community

## The development of British democracy

Democracy is a system of government where the whole adult population gets a say. This might be by direct voting or by choosing representatives to make decisions on their behalf. At the turn of the 19th century, Britain was not a democracy as we know it today. Although there were elections to select members of Parliament (MPs), only a small group of people could vote. They were men who were over 21 years of age and who owned a certain amount of property. The franchise (that is the number of people who had the right to vote) grew over the course of the 19th century and political parties began to involve ordinary men and women as members.

In the 1830s and 1840s, a group called the Chartists campaigned for reform. They wanted six changes:

• for every man to have the vote
• elections every year
• for all regions to be equal in the electoral system
• secret ballots • for any man to be able to stand as an MP
• for MPs to be paid At the time, the campaign was generally seen as failure.

However, by 1918 most of these reforms had been adopted. The voting franchise was also extended to women over 30, and then in 1928 to men and women over 21. In 1969, the voting age was reduced to 18 for men and women.

# The British constitution

A constitution is a set of principles by which a country is governed. It includes all of the institutions that are responsible for running the country and how their power is kept in check. The constitution also includes laws and conventions. The British constitution is not written down in any single document, and therefore it is described as 'unwritten'. This is mainly because the UK, unlike America or France, has never had a revolution which led permanently to a totally new system of government. Our most important institutions have developed over hundreds of years. Some people believe that there should be a single document, but others believe an unwritten constitution allows for more flexibility and better government.

# Constitutional institutions

In the UK, there are several different parts of government. The main ones are:

• the monarchy
• Parliament (the House of Commons and the House of Lords)
• the Prime Minister
• the cabinet
• the judiciary (courts)
• the police
• the civil service
• local government

In addition, there are devolved governments in Scotland, Wales and Northern Ireland that have the power to legislate on certain issues.

# The monarchy

Queen Elizabeth II is the head of state of the UK. She is also the monarch or head of state for many countries in the Commonwealth. The UK has a constitutional monarchy. This means that the king or queen does not rule the country but appoints the government, which the people have chosen in a democratic election. The monarch invites the leader of the party with the largest number of MPs or the leader of a coalition between more than one party, to become the Prime Minister. The monarch has regular meetings with the Prime Minister and can advise, warn and encourage, but the decisions on government policies are made by the Prime Minister and cabinet (see the section on 'The government').

The Queen has reigned since her father's death in 1952, and in 2012 she celebrated her Diamond Jubilee (60 years as queen). She is married to Prince Philip, the Duke of Edinburgh. Her eldest son, Prince Charles (the Prince of Wales), is the heir to the throne.

The Queen has important ceremonial roles, such as the opening of the new parliamentary session each year. On this occasion the Queen makes a speech which summarises the government's policies for the year ahead. All Acts of Parliament are made in her name.

The Queen represents the UK to the rest of the world. She receives foreign ambassadors and high commissioners, entertains visiting heads of state, and makes state visits overseas in support of diplomatic and economic relationships with other counties. The Queen has an important role in providing stability and continuity. While governments and Prime Ministers change regularly, the Queen continues as head of state. She provides a focus for national identity and pride, which was demonstrated through the celebrations of her Jubilee.

## The National Anthem

The National Anthem of the UK is 'God Save the Queen'. It is played at important national occasions and at events attended by the Queen or the Royal Family.

The first verse is: 'God save our gracious Queen! Long live our noble Queen! God save the Queen! Send her victorious, Happy and glorious, Long to reign over us, God save the Queen!'

New citizens swear or affirm loyalty to the Queen as part of the citizenship ceremony.

*Oath of allegiance*

I (name) swear by Almighty God that on becoming a British citizen, I will be faithful and bear true allegiance to Her Majesty Queen Elizabeth the Second, her Heirs and Successors, according to law.

*Affirmation of allegiance*

I (name) do solemnly, sincerely and truly declare and affirm that on becoming a British citizen, I will be faithful and bear true allegiance to Her Majesty Queen Elizabeth the Second, her Heirs and Successors, according to law.

## System of Government

The system of government in the UK is a parliamentary democracy. The UK is divided into parliamentary constituencies. Voters in each constituency elect their Member of Parliament (MP) in a General Election. All of the elected MPs form the House of Commons. Most MPs belong to a political party, and the party with the majority of MPs forms the government. If one party does not get a majority, two parties can join together to form a coalition.

# The House of Commons

The House of Commons is regarded as the more important of the two chambers in Parliament because its members are democratically elected. The Prime Minister and almost all the members of the cabinet are members of the House of Commons (MPs). Each MP represents a parliamentary constituency, which is a small area of the country. MPs have a number of different responsibilities. They:
• Represent everyone in their constituency
• Help to create new laws
• Scrutinize and comment on what the government is doing
• Debate important national issues

# The House of Lords

Members of the House of Lords, known as peers, are not elected by the people and do not represent a constituency. The role and membership of the House of Lords has changed over the last 50 years.

Until 1958, all peers were:

• 'hereditary', which means they inherited their title, or
• senior judges, or
• bishops of the Church of England.

Since 1958, the Prime Minister has had the power to nominate peers just for their own lifetime. These are called life peers. They have usually had an important career in politics, business, law or another profession. Life peers are appointed by the monarch on the advice of the Prime Minister. They also include people nominated by the leaders of the other main political parties or by an independent Appointments Commission for non-party peers. Since 1999, hereditary peers have lost the automatic right to attend the House of Lords. They now elect a few of their number to represent them in the House of Lords.

The House of Lords is normally more independent of the government than the House of Commons. It can suggest amendments or propose new laws, which are then discussed by MPs. The House of Lords checks laws that have been passed by the House of Commons to ensure they are fit for purpose. It also holds the government to account to make sure that it is working in the best interests of the people. There are peers who are specialists in particular areas, and their knowledge is useful in making and checking laws. The House of Commons has powers to overrule the House of Lords, but these are not used often.

The Speaker Debates in the House of Commons are chaired by the Speaker. This person is the chief officer of the House of Commons. The Speaker is neutral and does not represent a political party, even though he or she is an MP, represents a constituency and deals with the constituents' problems like any other MP. The Speaker is chosen by other MPs in a secret ballot. The Speaker keeps order during political debates to make sure the rules are followed. This includes making sure the opposition (see the section on 'The government') has a guaranteed amount of time to debate issues which it chooses. The Speaker also represents Parliament on ceremonial occasions.

## Elections

MPs are elected at a General Election, which is held at least every five years.

If an MP dies or resigns, there will be a fresh election, called a by-election, in his or her constituency. MPs are elected through a system called 'first past the post'. In each constituency, the candidate who gets the most votes is elected. The government is usually formed by the party that wins the majority of constituencies. If no party wins a majority, two parties may join together to form a coalition.

**Check that you understand**

**• How democracy has developed in the UK**
**• What a constitution is and how the UK's constitution is different from those of most other countries**
**• The role of the monarch**
**• The role of the House of Commons and House of Lords**
**• What the Speaker does**
**• How the UK elects MPs**

# The Prime Minister

The Prime Minister (PM) is the leader of the political party in power. He or she appoints the members of the cabinet (see below) and has control over many important public appointments. The official home of the Prime Minister is 10 Downing Street, in central London, near the Houses of Parliament. He or she also has a country house outside London called Chequers. The Prime Minister can be changed if the MPs in the governing party decide to do so, or if he or she wishes to resign. The Prime Minister usually resigns if his or her party loses a General Election.

# The cabinet

The Prime Minister appoints about 20 senior MPs to become ministers in charge of departments.

These include:
• Chancellor of the Exchequer – responsible for the economy
• Home Secretary – responsible for crime, policing and immigration
• Foreign Secretary - responsible for managing relationships with foreign countries

• Other ministers (called 'Secretaries of State') responsible for subjects such as education, health and defence. These ministers form the cabinet, a committee which usually meets weekly and makes important decisions about government policy. Many of the decisions have to be debated or approved by Parliament.

Each department also has a number of other ministers, called Ministers of State and Parliamentary Under-Secretaries of State, who take charge of particular areas of the department's work.

## The opposition

The second-largest party in the House of Commons is called the opposition. The leader of the opposition usually becomes Prime Minister if his of her party wins the next General Election. The leader of the opposition leads his or her party in pointing out what they see as the government's failures and weaknesses. One important opportunity to do this is at Prime Minister's Questions, which takes place every week while Parliament is sitting. The leader of the opposition also appoints senior opposition MPs to be 'shadow ministers'. They form the shadow cabinet and their role is to challenge the government and put forward alternative policies.

## The party system

Anyone aged 18 or over can stand for election as an MP but they are unlikely to win unless they have been nominated to represent one of the major political parties. These are the Conservative Party, the Labour Party, the Liberal Democrats, or one of the parties representing Scottish, Welsh or Northern Irish interests. There are a few MPs who do not represent any of the main political parties. They are called 'independents' and usually represent an issue important to their constituency. The main political parties actively look for members of the public to join their debates, contribute to their costs, and help at elections for Parliament or for local government. They have branches in most constituencies and hold policy-making conferences every year. Pressure and lobby groups are organisations which try to influence government policy. They play an important role in politics. Some are representative organisations such as the CBI (Confederation of British Industry), which represents the views of British business. Others campaign on particular topics, such as the environment (for example, Greenpeace) or human rights (for example, Liberty).

## The civil service

Civil servants support the government in developing and implementing its policies. They also deliver public services. Civil servants are accountable to ministers. They are chosen on merit and are politically neutral – they are not political appointees. People can apply to join the civil service through an application process, like other jobs in the UK. Civil servants are expected to carry out their role with dedication and a commitment to the civil service and its core values. These are: integrity, honesty, objectivity and impartiality (including being politically neutral).

## Local government

Towns, cities and rural areas in the UK are governed by democratically elected councils, often called 'local authorities'. Some areas have both district and county councils, which have different functions. Most large towns and cities have a single local authority.

Local authorities provide a range of services in their areas. They are funded by money from central government and by local taxes. Many local authorities appoint a mayor, who is the ceremonial leader of the council. In some towns, a mayor is elected to be the effective leader of the administration. London has 33 local authorities, with the Greater London Authority and the Mayor of London coordinating policies across the capital. For most local authorities, local elections for councillors are held in May every year. Many candidates stand for council election as members of a political party.

# Devolved administrations

Since 1997, some powers have been devolved from the central government to give people in Wales, Scotland and Northern Ireland more control over matters that directly affect them. There has been a Welsh Assembly and a Scottish Parliament since 1999. There is also a Northern Ireland Assembly, although this has been suspended on a few occasions. Policy and laws governing defence, foreign affairs, immigration, taxation and social security all remain under central UK government control. However, many other public services, such as education, are controlled by the devolved administrations. The devolved administrations each have their own civil service.

# The Welsh government

The Welsh government and National Assembly for Wales are based in Cardiff, the capital city of Wales. The National Assembly has 60 Assembly members (AMs) and elections are held every four years using a form of proportional representation. Members can speak in either Welsh or English, and all of the Assembly's publications are in both languages.

The Assembly has the power to make laws for Wales in 20 areas, including:

• education and training
• health and social services
• economic development
• housing.

Since 2011, the National Assembly for Wales has been able to pass laws on these topics without the agreement of the UK Parliament.

# The Scottish Parliament

The Scottish Parliament was formed in 1999. It sits in Edinburgh, the capital city of Scotland. There are 129 members of the Scottish Parliament (MSPs), elected by a form of proportional representation. The Scottish Parliament can pass laws for Scotland of all matters which are not specifically reserved to the UK Parliament.

The matters on which the Scottish Parliament can legislate include:

• Civil and criminal law
• Health
• Education
• Planning
• Additional tax-raising powers


## The Northern Ireland Assembly

A Northern Ireland Parliament was established in 1922, when Ireland was divided, but it was abolished in 1972, shortly after the Troubles broke out in 1969. The Northern Ireland Assembly was established soon after the Belfast Agreement (or Good Friday Agreement) in 1998. There is a power-sharing agreement which distributes ministerial offices amongst the main parties. The Assembly has 108 elected members, known as MLAs (members of the Legislative Assembly).

They are elected with a form of proportional representation. The Northern Ireland Assembly can make decisions on issues such as:

• education
• agriculture
• the environment
• health
• social services

The UK government has the power to suspend all devolved assemblies. It has used this power several times in Northern Ireland when local political leaders found it difficult to work together.

# The media and government

Proceedings in Parliament are broadcast on television and published in official reports called Hansard. Written reports can be found in large libraries and at www.parliament.uk. Most people get information about political issues and events from newspapers (often called 'the press'), television, radio and the internet. The UK has a free press. This means that what is written in newspapers is free from government control. Some newspaper owners and editors hold strong political opinions and run campaigns to try to influence government policy and public opinion. By law, radio and television coverage of the political parties must be balanced and so equal time has to be given to rival viewpoints.

**Check that you understand**

• **The role of the Prime Minister, cabinet, opposition and shadow cabinet.**
• **The role of political parties in the UK system of government**
• **Who the main political parties are**
• **What pressure and lobby groups do**
• **The role of the civil service**
• **The role of local government**
• **The powers of the devolved governments in Wales, Scotland and Northern Ireland**
• **How proceedings in Parliament are recorded**
• **The role of the media in keeping people informed about political issues**

# Who can vote?

The UK has had a fully democratic voting system since 1928. The present voting age of 18 was set in 1969 and (with a few exceptions) all UK-born and naturalised adult citizens have the right to vote. Adult citizens of the UK, and citizens of the Commonwealth and the Irish Republic who are resident in the UK, can vote in all public elections. Adult citizens of other EU states who are resident in the UK can vote in all elections except General Elections.

## The electoral register

To be able to vote, you can register by contacting your local council electoral registration office. This is usually based at your local council (in Scotland it may be based elsewhere). If you don't know which local authority you come under, you can find out by visiting www.aboutmyvote.co.uk and entering you postcode. You can also download voter registration forms in English, Welsh and some other languages.

 The electoral register is updated every year in September or October. An electoral registration form is sent to every household and this has to be completed and returned with the names of everyone who is resident in the household and eligible to vote. In Northern Ireland a different system operates. This is called 'individual registration' and all those entitled to vote must complete their own registration form. Once registered, people stay on the register provided their personal details do not change.

For more information see the Electoral Office for Northern Ireland website at www.eoni.org.uk By law, each local authority has to make its electoral register available for anyone to look at, although this has to be supervised. The register is kept at each local electoral registration office (or council office in England and Wales). It is also possible to see the register at some public buildings such as libraries.

## Where to vote

People vote in elections at places called polling stations, or polling places in Scotland. Before the election you will be sent a poll card. This tells you where your polling station or polling place is and when the election will take place. On election day, the polling station or place will be open from 7.00 am until 10.00 pm. When you arrive at the polling station, the staff will ask for your name and address. In Northern Ireland you will also have to show photographic identification.

You will then get your ballot paper, which you take to a polling booth to fill in privately. You should make up your own mind who to vote for. No one has the right to make you vote for a particular candidate.

You should follow the instructions on ballot paper. Once you have completed it, put it in the ballot box. If it is difficult for you to get to a polling station or polling place, you can register for a postal ballot. Your ballot paper will be sent to your home before the election. You then fill it in and post it back. You can choose to do this when you register to vote.

## Standing for office

Most citizens of the UK, the Irish republic or the Commonwealth aged 18 or over can stand for public office. There are some exceptions, including:

• Members of the armed forces
• Civil servants
• People found guilty of certain criminal offences.

Members of the House of Lords may not stand for election to the House of Commons but are eligible for all other public offices.

## The UK Parliament

The public can listen to debates in the Palace of Westminster from public galleries in both the House of Commons and the House of Lords. You can write to your local MP in advance to ask for tickets or you can Queue on the day at the public entrance. Entrance is free. Sometimes there are long queues for the House of Commons and people have to wait for at least one or two hours. It is usually easier to get in to the House of Lords.

**Check that you understand**

• **Who is eligible to vote**
• **How you register to vote**
• **How to vote**
• **Who can stand for public office**

# The UK and international institutions

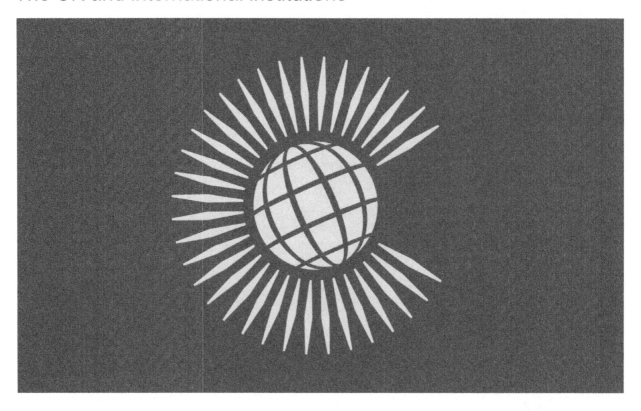

The Commonwealth is an association of countries that support each other and work together towards shared goals in democracy and development. Most member states were once part of the British Empire, although a few countries which were not have also joined. The Queen is the ceremonial head of the Commonwealth, which currently has 54 member states (see table below). Membership is voluntary.

| Commonwealth members | | |
| --- | --- | --- |
| Antigua and Barbuda | Australia | The Bahamas |
| Bangladesh | Barbados | Belize |
| Botswana | Brunei Darussalam | Cameroon |
| Canada | Cyprus | Dominica |
| Fiji (currently suspended) | The Gambia | Ghana |
| Grenada | Guyana | India |
| Jamaica | Kenya | Kiribati |
| Lesotho | Malawi | Malaysia |
| Maldives | Malta | Mauritius |

| Commonwealth members | | |
|---|---|---|
| Mozambique | Namibia | Nauru |
| New Zealand | Nigeria | Pakistan |
| Papua New Guinea | Rwanda | Samoa |
| Seychelles | Sierra Leone | Singapore |
| Solomon Islands | South Africa | Sri Lanka |
| St Kitts and Nevis | St Lucia | St Vincent and the Grenadines |
| Swaziland | Tanzania | Tonga |
| Trinidad and Tobago | Tuvalu | Uganda |
| UK | Vanuatu | Zambia |

## The European Union

The European Union (EU), originally called the European Economic Community (EEC), was set up by six western European countries (Belgium, France, Germany, Italy, Luxembourg and the Netherlands) who signed the Treaty of Rome on 25 March 1957. The UK originally decided not to join this group but it became a member in 1973. The United Kingdom voted to leave the EU in 2016 and officially left the union in 2020. The UK has several agreements with EU, particularly in relation to Northern Ireland which shares a border with the republic of Ireland, an EU member country.

## The Council of Europe

The Council of Europe is separate from the EU. It has 47 member countries, including the UK, and is responsible for the protection and promotion of human rights in those countries. It has no power to make laws but draws up conventions and charters, the most well-known of which is the European Convention on Human Rights and Fundamental Freedoms, usually called the European Convention on Human Rights.

## The United Nations

The UK is part of the United Nations (UN), an international organization with more than 190 countries as members. The UN was set up after the Second World War and aims to prevent war and promote international peace and security. There are 15 members on the UN Security

Council, which recommends action when there are international crises and threats to peace. The UK is one of five permanent members of the Security Council.

## The North Atlantic Treaty Organization (NATO)

The UK is also a member of NATO. NATO is a group of European and North American countries that have agreed to help each other if they come under attack. It also aims to maintain peace between all of its members.

**Check that you understand**

• **What the Commonwealth is and its role**
• **Other international organisations of which the UK is a member**

## Respecting the law

One of the most important responsibilities of all residents in the UK is to know and obey the law. This section will tell you about the legal system in the UK and some of the laws that may affect you. Britain is proud of being a welcoming country, but all residents, regardless of their background, are expected to comply with the law and to understand that some things which may be allowed in other legal systems are not acceptable in the UK. Those who do not respect the law should not expect to be allowed to become permanent residents of the UK. The law is relevant to all areas of life in the UK. You should make sure that you are aware of the laws which affect your everyday life, including both your personal and business affairs.

## The law in the UK

Every person in the UK receives equal treatment under the law. This means that the law applies in the same way to everyone, no matter who they are or where they are from. Laws can be divided into criminal law and civil law:

• Criminal law relates to crimes, which are usually investigated by the police or another authority such as a council, and which are punished by the courts.

• Civil law is used to settle disputes between individuals or groups.

Examples of criminal laws are:

• Carrying a weapon: it is a criminal offence to carry a weapon of any kind, even if it is for self-defence. This includes a gun, a knife or anything that is made or adapted to cause injury.

• Drugs: selling or buying drugs such as heroin, cocaine, ecstasy and cannabis is illegal in the UK.

• Racial crime: it is a criminal offence to cause harassment, alarm or distress to someone because of their religion or ethnic origin.

• Selling tobacco: it is illegal to sell tobacco products (for example, cigarettes, cigars, roll-up tobacco) to anyone under the age of 18.

• Smoking in public places: it is against the law to smoke tobacco products in nearly every enclosed public place in the UK. There are signs displayed to tell you where you cannot smoke.

• Buying alcohol: it is a criminal offence to sell alcohol to anyone who is under 18 or to buy alcohol for people who are under the age of 18.

• Drinking in public: some places have alcohol-free zones where you cannot drink in public. The police can also confiscate alcohol or move young people on from public places. You can be fined or arrested.

This list does not include all crimes. There are many that apply in most countries, such as murder, theft and assault. You can find out more about types of crime in the UK at www.gov.uk

Example of civil laws are:

• Housing law: this includes disputes between landlords and tenants over issues such as repairs and eviction.

• Consumer rights: an example of this is a dispute about faulty goods or services.

• Employment law: these cases include disputes over wages and cases of unfair dismissal or discrimination in the workplace.

• Debt: people might be taken to court if they owe money to someone.

The police and their duties

The job of the police in the UK is to:

• Protect life and property

• Prevent disturbances (also known as keeping the peace)
• Prevent and detect crime.

The police are organised into a number of separate police forces headed by Chief Constables. They are independent of the government. In November 2012, the public elected Police and Crime Commissioners (PCCs) in England and Wales. These are directly elected individuals who are responsible for the delivery of an efficient and effective police force that reflects the needs of their local communities. PCCs set local police priorities and the local policing budget. They also appoint the local Chief Constable.

The police force is a public service that helps and protects everyone, no matter what their background or where they live. Police officers must themselves obey the law. They must not misuse their authority, make a false statement, be rude or abusive, or commit racial discrimination.

If police officers corrupt or misuse their authority they are severely punished. Police officers are supported by the police community support officers (PCSOs). PCSOs have different roles according to the area but usually patrol the streets, work wth the public, and support police officers at crime scenes and major events.

All people in the UK are expected to help the police prevent and detect crimes whenever they can. If you are arrested and taken to a police station, a police officer will tell you the reason for your arrest and you will be able to seek legal advice.

If something goes wrong, the police complaints system tries to put it right. Anyone can make a complaint about the police by going to a police station and writing to the Chief Constable of the police force involved. Complaints can also be made to an independent body: the Independent Police Complaints Commission in England and Wales, the Police Complaints Commissioner for Scotland or the Police Ombudsman for Northern Ireland.

## Terrorism and extremism

The UK faces a range of terrorist threats. The most serious of these is from Al Qa'ida, its affiliates and like-minded organisations. The UK also faces threats from other kind of terrorism, such as Northern Ireland-related terrorism. All terrorist groups try to radicalise and recruit people to their cause. How, where and to what extent they try to do so will vary. Evidence shows that these groups attract very low levels of public support, but people who want to make their home in the UK should be aware of this threat. It is important that all citizens feel safe. This includes feeling safe from all kinds of extremism (vocal or active opposition to fundamental British values), including religious extremism and far-right extremism. If you think someone is trying to persuade you to join an extremist or terrorist cause, you should notify your local police force.

**Check that you understand**

• **The difference between civil and criminal law and some examples of each**
• **The duties of the police**
• **The possible terrorist threats facing the UK**

# The judiciary

Judges (who are together called 'the judiciary') are responsible for interpreting the law and ensuring that trials are conducted fairly. The government cannot interfere with this.

Sometimes the actions of the government are claimed to be illegal. If the judges agree, then the government must either change its policies or ask Parliament to change the law. If judges find that a public body is not respecting someone's legal rights, they can order that body to change its practices and/or pay compensation.

Judges also make decisions in disputes between members of the public or organisations. These might be about contracts, property or employment rights or after an accident.

# Criminal courts

There are some differences between the court systems in England and Wales, Scotland and Northern Ireland.

# Magistrates' and Justice of the Peace Courts

In England, Wales and Northern Ireland, most minor criminal cases are dealt with in a Magistrates' Court. In Scotland, minor criminal offences go to a Justice of the Peace Court. Magistrates and Justices of the Peace (JPs) are members of the local community. In England, Wales and Scotland they usually work unpaid and do not need legal qualifications. They receive training to do the job and are supported by a legal adviser. Magistrates decide the verdict in each case that comes before them and, if the person is found guilty, the sentence that they are given. In Northern Ireland, cases are heard by a District Judge or Deputy District Judge, who is legally qualified and paid.

# Crown Courts and Sheriff Courts

In England, Wales and Northern Ireland, serious offences are tried in front of a judge and a jury in a Crown Court. In Scotland, serious cases are heard in a Sheriff Court with either a sheriff or a sheriff with a jury. The most serious cases in Scotland, such as murder, are heard at a High Court with a judge and jury. A jury is made up of members of the public chosen at random from the local electoral register.

In England, Wales and Northern Ireland a jury has 12 members, and in Scotland a jury has 15 members. Everyone who is summoned to do jury service must do it unless they are not eligible (for example, because they have a criminal conviction) or they provide a good reason to be excused, such as ill health. The jury has to listen to the evidence presented at the trial and then decide a verdict of 'guilty' or 'not guilty' based of what they have heard. In Scotland, a third verdict of 'not proven' is also possible. If the jury finds a defendant guilty, the judge decides the penalty.

## Youth Courts

In England, Wales and Northern Ireland, if an accused person is aged 10 to 17, the case is normally heard in a Youth Court in front of up to three specially trained magistrates or a District Judge. The most serious cases will go to the Crown Court. The parents or carers of the young person are expected to attend the hearing. Members of the public are not allowed in Youth

Courts, and the name or photographs of the accused young person cannot be published in newspapers or used by the media.

In Scotland a system called the Children's Hearings System is used to deal with children and young people who have committed an offence. Northern Ireland has a system of youth conferencing to consider how a child should be dealt with when they have committed an offence.

# Civil Courts

County Courts deal with a wide range of civil disputes. These include people trying to get back money that is owed to them, cases involving personal injury, family matters, breaches of contract, and divorce. In Scotland, most of these matters are dealt with in the Sheriff Court. More serious civil cases – for example, when a large amount of compensation is being claimed – are dealt with in the High Court of England, Wales and Northern Ireland. In Scotland, they are dealt with in the Court of Session in Edinburgh.

# The small claims procedure

The small claims procedure is an informal way of helping people to settle minor disputes without spending a lot of time and money using a lawyer. This procedure is used for claims of less than £5,000 in England and Wales and £3,000 in Scotland and Northern Ireland. The hearing is held in front of a judge in an ordinary room, and people from both sides of the dispute sit around a table. Small claims can also be issued online through Money Claims Online (www.moneyclaim.gov.uk). You can get details about the small claims procedure from your local County Court or Sheriff Court.

# Legal Advice

Solicitors are trained lawyers who give advice on legal matters, take action for their clients and represent their clients in court. There are solicitors' offices throughout the UK. It is important to find out which aspects of law a solicitor specialises in and to check that they have the right experience to help you with your case. Many advertise in local newspapers and in Yellow Pages. The Citizens Advice Bureau (www.citizensadvice.org.uk) can give you names of local solicitors and which areas of law they specialise in. You can also get this information from the Law Society (www.lawsociety.org.uk) in England and Wales, the Law Society of Scotland (www.lawscot.org.uk) or the Law Society of Northern Ireland (www.lawsoc-ni.org). Solicitors' charges are usually based on how much time they spend of a case. It is very important to find out at the start how much a case is likely to cost.

**Check that you understand**

- **The role of the judiciary**
- **About the different criminal courts in the UK**
- **About the different civil courts in the UK**
- **How you can settle a small claim**

## Fundamental principles

Britain has a long history of respecting an individual's rights and ensuring essential freedoms. These rights have their roots in Magna Carta, the Habeas Corpus Act and the Bill of Rights of 1689, and they have developed over a period of time. British diplomats and lawyers had an important role in drafting the European Convention on Human Rights and Fundamental Freedoms. The UK was one of the first countries to sign the Convention in 1950.

Some of the principles included in the European Convention of Human Rights are:

- right to life
- prohibition of torture
- prohibition of slavery and forced labour
- right to liberty and security
- right to a fair trial
- freedom of thought, conscience and religion
- freedom of expression (speech).

The Human Rights Act 1998 incorporated the European Convention of Human Rights into UK law. The government, public bodies and the courts must follow the principles of the Convention.

Equal opportunities

UK laws ensure that people are not treated unfairly in any area of life or work because of their age, disability, sex, pregnancy and maternity, race, religion or belief, sexuality or marital status. If you face problems with discrimination, you can get more information from the Citizens Advice Bureau or from one of the following organisations:

- England and Wales: Equality and Human Rights Commission (www.equalityhumanrights.com)

- Scotland: Equality and Human Rights Commission in Scotland (www.equalityhumanrights.com/scotland/the-commission-in-scotland) and Scottish Human Rights Commission (www.scottishhumanrights.com)

- Northern Ireland: equality Commission for Northern Ireland (www.equalityni.org) • Northern Ireland Human Rights Commission (www.nihrc.org).

# Domestic violence

In the UK, brutality and violence in the home is a serious crime. Anyone who is violent towards their partner – whether they are a man or a woman, married or living together – can be prosecuted. Anyone who forces another person to have sex, including husbands, wives and civil partners, can be charged with rape.

It is important for anyone facing domestic violence to get help as soon as possible. A solicitor or the Citizens Advice Bureau can explain the available options.

# Female genital mutilation

Female genital mutilation (FGM), also known as cutting or female circumcision, is illegal in the UK. Practicing FGM or taking a girl or woman abroad for FGM is a criminal offence.

# Forced marriage

A marriage should be entered into with the full and free consent of both people involved. Arranged marriages, where both parties agree to the marriage, are acceptable in the UK.

Forced marriage is where one or both parties do not or cannot give their consent to enter into the partnership. Forcing another person to marry is a criminal offence. Forced Marriage Protection Orders were introduced in 2008 for England, Wales and Northern Ireland under the Forced Marriage (Civil Protection) Act 2007.

Court orders can be obtained to protect a person from being forced into a marriage, or to protect a person in a forced marriage. Similar Protection Orders were introduced in Scotland in November 2011. A potential victim, or someone acting for them, can apply for an order. Anyone found to have breached an order can be jailed for up to two years for contempt of court.

# Income Tax

Income tax People in the UK have to pay tax on their income, which includes: • Wages from paid employment • Profits from self-employment • Taxable benefits • Pensions • Income from property, savings and dividends. Money raised from income tax pays for government services such as roads, education, police and the armed forces. For most people, the right amount of income tax is automatically taken from their income from employment by their employer and paid directly to HM Revenue & Customs (HMRC), the government department that collects taxes. This system is called "Pay As You Earn" (PAYE). If you are self-employed, you need to pay your own tax through a system called 'self-assessment', which includes completing a tax return. Other people may also need to complete a tax return. If HMRC sends you a tax return, it is important to complete and return the form as soon as you have all the necessary information.

# National Insurance

Almost everybody in the UK who is in paid work, including self-employed people, must pay National Insurance Contributions. The money raised from National Insurance Contributions is used to pay for state benefits and services such as the state retirement pension and the National Health Service (NHS).

Employees have their National Insurance Contributions deducted from their pay by their employer. People who are self-employed need to pay National Insurance Contributions themselves. Anyone who does not pay enough National Insurance Contributions will not be able to receive certain contributory benefits such as Jobseeker's Allowance or a full state retirement pension. Some workers, such as part-time workers, may not qualify for statutory payments such as maternity pay if they do not earn enough.

# Getting a National Insurance number

A National Insurance number is a unique personal account number. It makes sure that the National Insurance Contributions and tax you pay are properly recorded against your name. All young people in the UK are sent a National Insurance number just before their 16th birthday. A non-UK national living in the UK and looking for work, starting work or setting up as self-employed will need a National Insurance number.

However, you can start work without one. If you have permission to work in the UK, you will need to telephone the Department for Work and Pensions (DWP) to arrange to get a National Insurance number. You may be required to attend an interview. The DWP will advise you of the appropriate application process and tell you which documents you will need to bring to an interview if one is necessary. You will usually need documents that prove your identity and that you have permission to work in the UK. A National Insurance number does not on its own prove to an employer that you have the right to work in the UK.

# Driving

In the UK, you must be at least 17 years to drive a car or motor cycle and you must have a driving licence to drive on public roads. To get a UK driving licence you must pass a driving test, which tests both your knowledge and your practical skills. You need to be at least 16 years old to ride a moped, and there are other age requirements and special tests for driving large vehicles. Drivers can use their driving licence until they are 70 years old. After that, the licence is valid for three years at a time. In Northern Ireland, a newly qualified driver must display an 'R' plate (for restricted driver) for one year after passing the test. If your driving licence if from a country in the European Union (EU), Iceland, Liechtenstein or Norway, you can drive in the UK for as long as your licence is valid.

If you have a licence from any other country, you may use it in the UK for up to 12 months. To continue driving after that, you must get a UK full driving licence. If you are resident in the UK, your car or motor cycle must be registered at the Driver and Vehicle Licensing Agency (DVLA). You must pay an annual road tax and display the tax disc, which shows that the tax has been paid, on the windowscreen.

You must also have valid motor insurance. It is a serious criminal offence to drive without insurance. If your vehicle is over three years old, you must take it to the Ministry of Transport (MOT) test every year. It is an offense not to have a MOT certificate if your vehicle is more than three years old.

**Check that you understand**

• **The fundamental principle of UK law**
• **That domestic violence, FGM and forced marriage are illegal in the UK**
• **The system of income tax and National Insurance**
• **The requirements for driving a car**

## Your role in the community

Becoming a British citizen or settling in the UK brings responsibilities but also opportunities. Everyone has the opportunity to participate in their community. This section looks at some of the responsibilities of being a citizen and gives information about how you can help to make your community a better place to live and work. Values and responsibilities Although Britain is one of the world's most diverse societies, there is a set of shared values and responsibilities that everyone can agree with.

These values and responsibilities include:
• To obey and respect the law
• To be aware of the rights of others and respect those rights
• To treat others with fairness
• To behave responsibly
• To help and protect your family
• To respect and preserve the environment
• To treat everyone equally, regardless of sex, race, religion, age, disability, class or sexual orientation
• To work to provide for yourself and your family
• To help others
• To vote in local and national government elections. Taking on these values and responsibilities will make it easier for you to become a full and active citizen.

# Being a good neighbour

When you move into a new house or apartment, introduce yourself to the people who live near you. Getting to know your neighbours can help you to become part of the community and make friends. Your neighbours are also a good source of help – for example, they may be willing to feed your pets if you are away, or offer advice on local shops and services. You can help prevent any problems and conflicts with your neighbours by respecting their privacy and limiting how much noise you make. Also try to keep your garden tidy, and only put your refuse bags and bins on the street or in communal areas if they are due to be collected.

# Getting involved in local activities

Volunteering and helping your community are an important part of being a good citizen. They enable you to integrate and get to know other people. It helps to make your community a better place if residents support each other. It also helps you to fulfil your duties as a citizen, such as behaving responsibly and helping others.

# Helping in schools

If you have children, there are many ways in which you can help at their schools. Parents can often help in classrooms, by supporting activities or listening to children read. Many schools organise events to raise money for extra equipment or out-of school activities. Activities might include book sales, toy sales or bringing food to sell. You might have good ideas of your own for raising money. Sometimes events are organised by parent-teacher associations (PTAs). Volunteering to help with their events or joining the association is a way of doing something good for the school and also making new friends in your local community. You can find out about these opportunities from notices in the school or notes your children bring home.

# School governors and school boards

School governors, or members of the school board in Scotland, are people from the local community who wish to make a positive contribution to their children's education. They must be aged 18 or over at the date of their election or appointment. There is no upper age limit. Governors and school boards have an important part to play in raising school standards. They have three key roles:

• Setting the strategic direction of the school
• Ensuring accountability
• Monitoring and evaluating school performance.

You can contact your local school to ask if they need a new governor or school board member. In England, you can also apply online at the School Governors' One-Stop Shop at www.sgoss.org.uk In England, parents and other community groups can apply to open a free school in their local area.

## Supporting political parties

Political parties welcome new members. Joining one is a way to demonstrate your support for certain views and to get involved in the democratic process. Political parties are particularly busy at election times. Members work hard to persuade people to vote for their candidates – for instance, by handing out leaflets in the street or by knocking on people's doors and asking for their support.

This is called 'canvassing'. You don't have to tell a canvasser how you intend to vote if you don't want to.

## Helping with local services

There are opportunities to volunteer with a wide range of local service providers, including local hospitals and youth projects. Services often want to involve local people in decisions about the way in which they work. Universities, housing associations, museums and arts councils may advertise for people to serve as volunteers in their governing bodies. You can volunteer with the police, and become a special constable or a lay (non-police) representative. You can also apply to become a magistrate. You will often find advertisements for vacancies in your local newspaper or on local radio.

## Blood and organ donation

Donated blood is used by hospitals to help people with a wide range of injuries and illnesses.

Giving blood only takes about an hour to do. You can register to give blood at:
• England and North Wales: www.blood.co.uk
• Rest of Wales: www.welsh-blood.org.uk
• Scotland: www.scotblood.co.uk
• Northern Ireland: www.nibts.org

Many people in the UK are waiting for organ transplants. If you register to be an organ donor, it can make it easier for your family to decide whether to donate your organs when you die. You can register to be an organ donor at www.organdonation.nhs.uk. Living people can also donate a kidney.

## Other ways to volunteer

Volunteering is working for good causes without payment. There are many benefits to volunteering, such as meeting new people and helping make your community a better place. Some volunteer activities will give you a chance to practise your English or develop work skills that will help you find or improve your curriculum vitae (CV). Many people volunteer simply because they want to help other people.

Activities you can do as a volunteer include:

• working with animals – for example, caring for animals at a local rescue shelter
• youth work – for example, volunteering at a youth group
• helping improve the environment – for example, participating in a litter pick-up in the local area
• working with the homeless in, for example, a homelessness shelter
• mentoring – for example, supporting someone who has just come out of prison
• work in health and hospitals – for example, working on an information desk in a hospital
• helping older people at, for example, a residential care home.

There are thousands of active charities and voluntary organizations in the UK. They work to improve the lives of people, animals and the environment in many different ways. They range from the British Red Cross, to small local charities working in particular areas. They include charities working with older people (such as Age UK), with children (for example, the National Society for the Prevention of Cruelty to Children (NSPCC)), and with the homeless (for example, Crisis and Shelter). There are also medical research charities (for example, Cancer Research UK), environmental charities (including the National Trust and Friends of the Earth) and charities working with animals (such as the People's Dispensary for Sick Animals (PDSA)). Volunteers are needed to help with their activities and to raise money. The charities often advertise in local newspapers, and most have websites that include information about their opportunities. You can also get information about volunteering for different organisations from www.do-it.org.uk There are many opportunities for younger people to volunteer and receive accreditation which will help them to develop their skills. These include the National Citizen Service programme, which gives 16- and 17-year-olds the opportunity to enjoy outdoor activities, develop their skills and take part in a community project.

You can find out more about these opportunities as follows:

• National Citizen Service: at nationalcitizenservice.direct.gov.uk
• England: at www.vinspired.com

• Wales: at www.gwirvol.org
• Scotland: at www.vds.org.uk
• Northern Ireland: at www.volunteernow.co.uk

# Looking after the environment

It is important to recycle as much of your waste as you can. Using recycled materials to make new products uses less energy and means that we do not need to extract more raw materials from the earth. It also means that less rubbish is created, so the amount being put into landfill is reduced. You can learn more about recycling and it benefits at www.recyclenow.com. At this website you can also find out what you can recycle at home and in the local area you live in England. This information is available for Wales at www.wasteawarenesswales.org.uk, for Scotland at www.recycleforscotland.com and for Northern Ireland from your local authority.

A good way to support your local community is to shop for products locally where you can. This will help businesses and farmers in your area in Britain. It will also reduce your carbon footprint, because the products you buy will not have had to travel as far.

Walking and using public transport to get around when you can is also a good way to protect the environment. It means that you create less pollution than when you use a car.

**Check that you understand**

• **The different ways you can help at your child's school**
• **The role of school governors and members of school boards, and how you can become one** • **The role of members of political parties**
• **The different local services people can volunteer to support**
• **How to donate blood and organs**
• **The benefit of volunteering for you, other people and the community**
• **The types of activities that volunteers can do**
• **How you can look after the environment**

# Practice Tests

## Practice Test 1

Q.1 What festival is celebrated on 31 October?
A Valentine's Day
B Bonfire Night
C Halloween
D Hogmanay

Q.2 Is the statement below TRUE or FALSE?
The British constitution is contained in a single written document.

Q.3 Which of the following statements is correct?
A EastEnders and Coronation Street are popular television programmes.
B EastEnders and Coronation Street are historical landmarks.

Q.4 In 1999, what happened to hereditary peers in the House of Lords?
A Their numbers were greatly increased.
B Their salaries were stopped.
C Women were allowed to inherit their titles.
D They lost their automatic right to attend the House of Lords.

Q.5 Is the statement below TRUE or FALSE?

Pantomimes are plays based on fairy stories.

Q.6 Which TWO are political parties in the UK ?
A Office Party
B Modern Party
C Conservative Party
D Labour Party

Q.7 How often does Prime Minister's Questions occur when Parliament is sitting?
A Every day
B Twice a week
C Once a week
D Once a month

Q.8 Which of the following statements is correct?

A The small claims procedure is an informal way of helping people to settle minor disputes.

B The small claims procedure helps people to make small home insurance claims.

Q.9 Which TWO are Protestant Christian groups in the UK?
A Baptists
B Methodists
C Roman Catholics
D Buddhists

Q.10 What are TWO fundamental principles of British life?
A Only driving your car on weekdays
B Participation in community life
C Growing your own fruit and vegetables
D Tolerance of those with different faiths and beliefs

Q.11 Why is 1918 an important date in the history of women's rights?

A The first divorce laws were introduced.
B Women were given the right to vote.
C Equal pay laws were passed.
D Women were made legally responsible for their children.

Q.12 Is the statement below TRUE or FALSE?

The National Citizen Service provides military training to young people.

Q.13 For which TWO types of literature is William Shakespeare famous?

A Novels
B Plays
C Biographies
D Sonnets

Q. 14 Which of the following statements is correct?

A In 1588 the English defeated a Spanish invasion fleet of ships.
B In 1588 the English defeated a German invasion fleet of bomber planes.

Q.15 What is the name of the UK currency?

A Dollar
B Euro
C Pound sterling
D Yen

Q.16 Which TWO are members of Parliament (MPs) responsible for?

A Representing everyone in their constituency
B Scrutinising and commenting on what the government is doing
C Representing only those who voted for them
D Supporting the government on all decisions and laws

Q.17 Which of the following statements is correct?
A Most shops in the UK open seven days a week.
B All shops in the UK close on Sundays.

Q.18 Which TWO are English Civil War battles?
A Waterloo
B Marston Moor
C Hastings
D Naseby

Q.19 Which of the following statements is correct?
A Mary, Queen of Scots was unrelated to Queen Elizabeth I.
B Mary, Queen of Scots was a cousin of Queen Elizabeth I.

Q.20 Is the statement below TRUE or FALSE ?
British scientists were the first to clone a mammal successfully.
The animal was a rabbit.

Q.21 Which TWO of the following do pressure and lobby groups do?
A Organise violent protests
B Influence government policy
C Assist MPs in their constituency work
D Represent the views of British businesses

Q.22 Is the statement below TRUE or FALSE?
There is a dragon on the official flag of Wales.

Q.23 What were the names of the TWO main groups in Parliament in the early 18th century?
A Whigs
B Labour
C Nationalists
D Tories

Q.24 Which stories are associated with Geoffrey Chaucer?
A The Westbury Tales
B The Ambridge Tales
C The London Tales
D The Canterbury Tales

# Practice Test 2

Q1.  What important change to our voting rights took place in 1969?
A  Women over 35 were given the vote.
B  Prisoners were given the vote.
C  The voting age was reduced to 18 for men and women.
D  Compulsory voting was introduced.

Q2.  Which TWO of the following are Christian religious festivals celebrated in the UK?
A  Easter
B  Halloween
C  Christmas
D New Year

Q3. Which of the following statements is correct?

A  Self-employed people need to pay National Insurance Contributions themselves.
B  Self-employed people can ask a friend to pay their National Insurance contributions on their behalf.

Q4.  How are local councils funded?
A  Through money raised from local fundraising events
B  Through donations from local people
C  From central government and local taxes
D  From local businesses

Q5.  Which of the following statements is correct?
A  Both Jane Austen and Charles Dickens are famous novelists.
B  Both Jane Austen and Charles Dickens are famous painters.

Q6.  What type of government was formed after the General Election of 2010?
A  National
B  All-party
C  One-party
D  Coalition

Q7.  Which is an aim of the United Nations?
A  To create a single free trade market
B  To prevent war and promote international peace and security

C  To examine decisions made by the European Union
D  To promote dictatorship

Q8.  Which of the following statements is correct?
A  The UK is governed by the parliament sitting in Westminster.
B  The UK is governed by parliaments sitting in Scotland, Wales and Northern Ireland.

Q9.  Is the statement below TRUE or FALSE?
*The Brit Awards is an event where sports people are given awards*

Q10.  What important event happened in England in 1066?
A  The Romans left England
B  The building of the Off a Dyke
C  The Norman invasion
D  The Battle of Bannockburn

Q11.  Which of the following statements is correct?
A  The Divine Right of Kings' meant that the English king should rule France.
B  The Divine Right of Kings' meant that the king was appointed by God.

Q12.  Which of the following is a fundamental principle of British life?
A  Extremism
B  Individual liberty
C  Intolerance
D  Inequality

Q13.  Which TWO are famous UK landmarks?
A  Snowdonia
B  Grand Canyon
C  Loch Lomond
D Notre Dame

Q14.  Is the statement below TRUE or FALSE?
*Members of the public are allowed to attend Youth Court hearings.*

Q15.  Which of the following statements is correct?
A  Elizabeth I handled Parliament very badly during her reign.
B  Elizabeth I had very good relations with Parliament.

Q16.  What event is remembered on 5 November each year?
A  The end of the Second World War
B  The Queen's birthday
C  A plot to blow up the Houses of Parliament in 1605
D  The defeat of the Spanish Armada in 1588

Q17. Which TWO were associated with King Charles I and Parliament during the English Civil War?
A Tories
B Roundheads
C Cavaliers
D Luddites

Q18. Is the statement below TRUE or FALSE?
*The Restoration' refers to the re-establishment of Catholicism as the official Church in the 17th century.*

Q19. Which TWO are examples of civil law?
A Disputes between landlords and tenants
B Carrying a weapon
C Discrimination in the workplace
D Selling tobacco

Q20. Is the statement below TRUE or FALSE?

*The Scottish Parliament can pass legislation for Scotland on all matters.*

Q21. Which of the following statements is correct?
A Gilbert and Sullivan were a comedy double act.
B Gilbert and Sullivan wrote many comic operas.

Q22. In 1999 which TWO new national bodies were established?
A House of Lords
B Welsh Assembly
C Scottish Parliament
D English Parliament

Q23. Is the statement below TRUE or FALSE?
*The Union Flag comprises four crosses, one for each part of the United Kingdom.*

Q24. Is the statement below TRUE or FALSE?
*Some people rent land called 'an allotment', where they grow fruit and vegetables.*

# Practice Test 3

Q1.Is the statement below TRUE or FALSE?
People are able to buy National Lottery tickets in the UK if they are aged 14 or over.

Q2.  Why was Magna Carta important?
A  It gave all men the vote.
B  It limited the power of the monarch.
C  It established a new system of free education.
D  It gave women legal rights.

Q3.  Which TWO types of case are held in County Courts?
A  Divorce
B  Murder
C  Minor criminal offences
D  Breaches of contract

Q4.  Which of the following statements is correct?
A  The Industrial Revolution was the rapid development of industry in the 18th and 19th centuries.
B  The Industrial Revolution introduced changes in the banking system in the 1970s.

Q5.  Who built the Tower of London?
A  Oliver Cromwell
B  Queen Elizabeth II
C  William the Conqueror
D  Winston Churchill

Q6.  Which TWO chambers form the UK Parliament?
A  House of Fraser
B  House of Lords
C  House of Commons
D  House of Representatives

Q7.  Which of the following statements is correct?
A  There is a yearly sailing race on the River Thames between Oxford and Cambridge Universities.
B  There is a yearly rowing race on the River Thames between Oxford and Cambridge Universities.

Q8.  Which TWO are plays by William Shakespeare?
A  A Midsummer Night's Dream

B  Pride and Prejudice
C  Romeo and Juliet
D  Oliver Twist

Q9.  Is the statement below TRUE or FALSE?
In 1805 at the Battle of Trafalgar, Admiral Nelson defeated the German fleet.

Q10.  Which TWO issues can the devolved administrations pass laws on?
A  Health
B  Education
C  Foreign affairs
D  Immigration

Q11.  Which of the following statements is correct?
A  UK laws ensure people are not treated unfairly in any area of work or life.
B  In the UK, employers can discriminate against different groups of people.

Q12.  Is the statement below TRUE or FALSE?
Wales united with England during the reign of Henry VIII.

Q13.  Which TWO are Christian groups?
A  Roman Catholics
B  Buddhists
C  Sikhs
D  Baptists

Q14.  What TWO freedoms are offered by the UK to citizens and permanent residents?
A Long lunch breaks on Friday
B Freedom of speech
C Free groceries for everyone
D A right to a fair trial

Q15. When is a by-election for a parliamentary seat held?
A Half-way through a parliamentary term
B Every two years
C When a member of Parliament (MP) dies or resigns
D When the Prime Minister decides to call one

Q16.  Which of the following statements is correct?
A  Volunteering is a good way to earn additional money.
B  Volunteering is a way of helping others without receiving payment.

Q17.  Which is the most popular sport in the UK?
A  Football

B  Rugby
C  Golf
D  Tennis

Q18.  Which of the following statements is correct?
A  Charles, king of Scotland, was restored as King Charles II of England in 1660.
B  Bonnie Prince Charlie became King Charles II of England in 1660.

Q19.  Which TWO of the following do you have to pay tax on?
A  Profits from self-employment
B  Income from property, savings and dividends
C  Shopping vouchers given to you by family or friends
D  Small amounts of money given to you as a gift

Q20.  Which of the following statements is correct?
A  The Proms is an eight-week summer season of orchestral music.
B  The Proms are a series of tennis matches held every June in London.

Q21.  What were 'the Troubles' about?
A  Independence for Wales
B  Disagreement over Ireland becoming one country
C  Independence for Scotland
D  Setting up an English Parliament

Q22.  Which TWO fought in wars against Napoleon?
A Margaret Thatcher
B Horatio Nelson
C  Winston Churchill
D  The Duke of Wellington

Q23.  Is the statement below TRUE or FALSE?
Most people in the UK live in towns and cities.

Q24.  What must you have done in order to vote in elections?
A  Paid income tax in the previous year
B  Put your name on the electoral register
C  Registered your identity with the police
D  Passed an electoral test

## Answers to Practice Test 1

| | ANSWER | EXPLANATION |
|---|---|---|
| **1** | C | Halloween is celebrated on 31 October. |
| **2** | FALSE | The British constitution is not written down in any single document and therefore it is described as 'unwritten'. |
| **3** | A | Popular television programmes include regular soap operas such as *EastEnders* and *Coronation Street*. |
| **4** | D | Hereditary peers are members of the House of Lords who have inherited their titles. In 1999 they lost their automatic right to attend and now only a few are left. |
| **5** | TRUE | Pantomime plays are a British tradition. Many theatres produce a pantomime at Christmas time. They are based on fairy stories and are light-hearted plays with music and comedy. |
| **6** | C and D | The major political parties in the UK include the Conservative Party, the Labour Party and the Liberal Democrats. |
| **7** | C | Prime Minister's Questions takes place every week while Parliament is sitting. |

**8** A     The small claims procedure is an informal way of helping people to settle minor disputes without spending a lot of time and money using a lawyer.

**9** A and B     Baptists and Methodists are Protestant Christian groups Other Protestant groups in the UK include the Church of England, the Church of Scotland, Presbyterians and Quakers.

**10** B and D     Participation in community life and tolerance of those with different faiths and beliefs are fundamental principles of British life. British society is founded on fundamental values and principles, which all those living in the UK should respect and support.

**11** B     In 1918, women over the age of 30 were given the right to vote. In 1928, women were given the right to vote at 21, the same age as men.

**12** FALSE     The National Citizen Service gives 16- and 17-year-olds the opportunity to enjoy outdoor activities, develop their skills and take part in a community project.

**13** B and D     William Shakespeare was a famous playwright and sonnet writer.

**14** A     The Spanish Armada (a large fleet of ships) attempted to invade England and restore Catholicism.

**15** C     The currency in the UK is the pound sterling. There are 100 pence in a pound.

**16**  A and B   MPs have a number of different responsibilities, including representing everyone in their constituency, and scrutinising and commenting on what the government is doing.

**17**  A   Most shops in the UK open seven days a week, although trading hours on Sundays and public holidays are generally reduced.

**18**  B and D   The Battles of Marston Moor and Naseby during the English Civil War were both won by the parliamentary armies.

**19**  B   Mary, Queen of Scots was a cousin of Queen Elizabeth I. Mary was executed on Elizabeth's orders, for plotting against her.

**20**  FALSE   The British team used a sheep for the first mammal cloning. The sheep was called Dolly.

**21**  B and D   Pressure groups and lobby groups play an important part in the UK political process. Groups such as the Confederation of British Industry (CBI – which represents British business) and Greenpeace (which is concerned about environmental issues) lobby politicians to get their views across.

**22**  TRUE   Wales has its own flag, which includes a dragon. The Welsh flag is not a part of the Union Flag, as Wales had united with England many years before the Union Flag was designed.

**23**  A and D   From 1689 onwards there were two main groups in Parliament, known as the Whigs and the Tories.

**24**  D   *The Canterbury Tales* are stories about a group of pilgrims travelling to Canterbury.

## Answers to Practice Test 2

| | ANSWER | EXPLANATION |
|---|---|---|
| **1** | C | In 1969, the voting age was reduced to 18 for men and women. |
| **2** | A and C | Easter and Christmas are two Christian festivals. Christmas celebrates the birth of Jesus Christ, and Easter marks his death on Good Friday and his rising from the dead on Easter Sunday. |
| **3** | A | Almost everybody in the UK who is in paid work must pay National Insurance Contributions. People who are self-employed must pay their own National Insurance Contributions. |
| **4** | C | Towns, cities and rural areas in the UK are governed by democratically elected councils, often called 'local authorities'. These are funded by money from central government and by local taxes. |
| **5** | A | Jane Austen and Charles Dickens are famous novelists. Jane Austen's books include *Pride and Prejudice* and *Sense and Sensibility*. Charles Dickens' novels include *Oliver Twist* and *Great Expectations*. |
| **6** | D | The 2010 coalition was formed by the Conservative and Liberal Democrat parties. |

**7**  B  The UK is part of the United Nations (UN), an international organisation with more than 190 countries as members. The UN was set up after the Second World War and aims to prevent war and promote international peace and security.

**8**  A  The UK is governed by the parliament sitting in Westminster. Scotland, Wales and Northern Ireland also have parliaments or assemblies of their own, with devolved powers in defined areas.

**9**  FALSE  The Brit Awards is an annual event that gives awards to musicians in a range of categories, such as best British group and best British solo artist.

**10**  C  William of Normandy invaded England in 1066 and defeated Harold, the Saxon king of England, at the Battle of Hastings.

**11**  B  King Charles I believed that monarchs should be able to rule without approval from Parliament. This principle was one factor that led to the English Civil War in 1642.

**12**  B  Individual liberty is a fundamental principle of British life. British society is founded on fundamental values and principles, which all those living in the UK should respect and support.

**13**  A and C  Snowdonia is a national park in North Wales. Loch Lomond is in the Trossachs National Park in the west of Scotland.

**14** FALSE    Members of the public are not allowed in Youth Courts, and the name or photographs of the accused young person cannot be published in newspapers or used by the media.

**15** B    Elizabeth managed her relationship with Parliament skilfully. Her successor James I and his son Charles I were far less skilful in their handling of Parliament.

**16** C    In 1605 a group of Catholics led by Guy Fawkes failed in their plan to kill the Protestant king with a bomb in the Houses of Parliament. The event is celebrated today as Bonfire Night.

**17** B and C    Supporters of the king were known as Cavaliers and supporters of Parliament were known as Roundheads.

**18** FALSE    The Restoration' refers to the re-establishment of the monarchy in 1660, when Charles II returned from exile after being invited back by Parliament.

**19** A and C    Civil law is used to settle disputes between individuals or groups. Examples of civil law include housing law, employment law, consumer rights and laws related to the recovery of debt.

**20** FALSE    The Scottish Parliament can pass laws for Scotland on all matters that are not specifically reserved to the UK Parliament.

**21** B    Gilbert and Sullivan wrote comic operas, such as *HMS Pinafore, The Pirates of Penzance* and *The Mikado*.

| 22 | B and C | Since 1997, some power has been devolved from central government. In 1999 the Scottish Parliament and the Welsh Assembly were established, to give people in Scotland and Wales more control over matters directly affecting them. |
| 23 | FALSE | The Union Flag comprises three crosses – the crosses of St George (England), St Andrew (Scotland) and St Patrick (Ireland). |
| 24 | TRUE | Allotments are plots of land that can be rented for growing fruit and vegetables. |

## Answers to Practice Test 3

| | ANSWER | EXPLANATION |
| --- | --- | --- |
| 1 | FALSE | People under 16 are not allowed to participate in the National Lottery. |
| 2 | B | King John was forced by his noblemen to agree to the Magna Carta, which restricted the power of the monarchy. |
| 3 | A and D | County Courts deal with a wide range of civil disputes, including divorce and other family matters, and breaches of contract. |
| 4 | A | The development of machinery transformed industries such as manufacturing and mining, and gave the UK industrial leadership from the early 18th century until the end of the 19th century. |

**5**    C      The Tower of London was built by William the Conqueror after he became king in 1066.

**6**    B and C      The UK Parliament is formed by the House of Commons and the House of Lords.

**7**    B      Rowing is a popular sport in the UK, both as a leisure activity and as a competitive sport. There is a popular yearly race on the River Thames between Oxford and Cambridge Universities.

**8**    A and C      Among the many plays that Shakespeare wrote are *A Midsummer Night's Dream* and *Romeo and Juliet*.

**9**    FALSE      At the Battle of Trafalgar in 1805 Admiral Nelson defeated a combined French and Spanish fleet. He was killed during the battle.

**10**    A and B      The devolved administrations in Scotland, Wales and Northern Ireland can pass laws on matters that directly affect them, including health and education.

**11**    A      UK laws ensure people are not treated unfairly in any area of life or work because of their age, disability, sex, pregnancy and maternity, race, religion or belief, sexuality or marital status.

**12**    TRUE      By the Act for the Government of Wales during the reign of King Henry VIII, Wales united with England.

**13**    A and D      Roman Catholics and Baptists are Christian groups. Baptists are a Protestant Christian group. Other Protestant groups include the Church of England, Methodists, Presbyterians and Quakers.

**14** B and D — There are responsibilities and freedoms which are shared by all those living in the UK. This includes freedom of speech and a right to a fair trial.

**15** C — If an MP dies or resigns, there will be a fresh election, called a by-election, in his or her constituency.

**16** B — Volunteering is working for good causes without payment. There are many activities you can do as a volunteer, such as working with the homeless and helping improve the environment.

**17** A — Football is the UK's most popular sport. It has a long history in the UK and the first professional football clubs were formed in the late 19th century.

**18** A — Charles II, whose father Charles I was executed at the end of the Civil War, was made king of Scotland by the Scots. He was forced into exile after being defeated by the English, but was restored to the throne of England in 1660 after the collapse of the republican Commonwealth.

**19** A and B — People in the UK have to pay tax on their income, which includes profits from self-employment, and income from property, savings and dividends. Money raised from income tax pays for government services such as roads, education, police and the armed forces.

**20** A     The Proms is an eight-week summer season of orchestral classical music. It has been organised by the British Broadcasting Corporation (BBC) since 1927.

**21** B     The Troubles' is a term used to describe the conflict that has occurred in Ireland between those who wish the North and South of Ireland to unite and those who wish the North to remain British.

**22** B and D     Admiral Lord Nelson commanded the British fleet at the Battle of Trafalgar in 1805. He died during the battle. The Duke of Wellington defeated Napoleon at the Battle of Waterloo in 1815.

**23** TRUE     Most people in the UK live in towns and cities but much of Britain is still countryside.

**24** B     To be able to vote in a parliamentary, local or European election, you must have your name on the electoral register. You can register by contacting your local council electoral registration office.

# Revision Crosswords

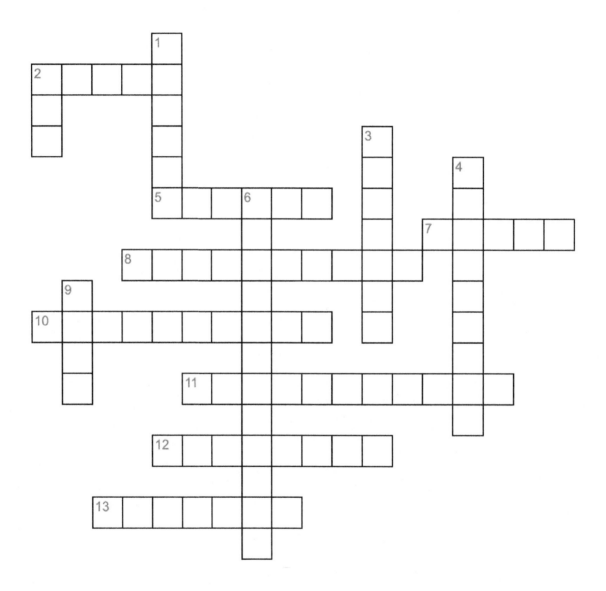

**Across**

2 One achievement of King James' reign was a new translation of the...

5 Was in charge of the British fleet at Trafalgar and was killed in the battle

7 Known in Scotland as 'The Bard'

8 Invented the cash-dispensing ATM (automatic teller machine) or 'cashpoint'

10 A charter of rights

11 Credited with the elevation of nursing practices

12 She reigned until 1901, almost 64 years

13 Opened the first curry house in Britain

**Down**

1 His most famous published work was Philosophiae Naturalis Principia Mathematica

2 The UK's national broadcaster

3 The first British Prime Minister

4 Became Prime Minister in 1940

6 Emmeline Pankhurst was the head of which group?

9 The last wife of Henry VIII

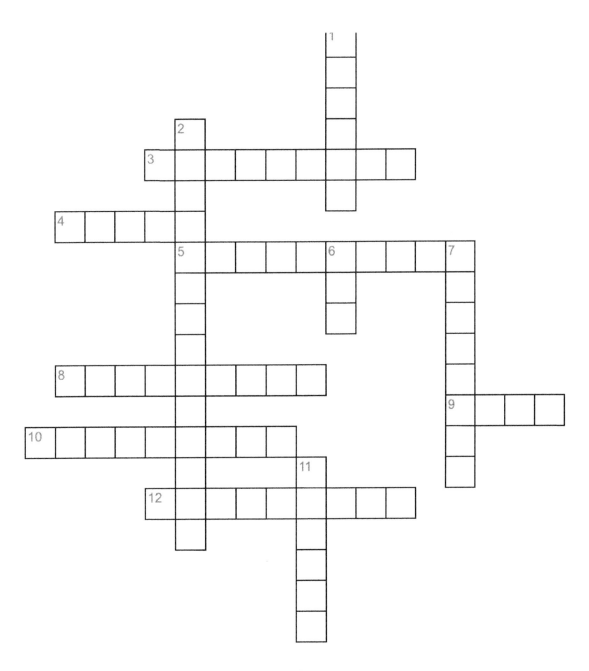

## Across

3  Celebrated on the 26th December
4  A cricket competition
5  Popular soap opera in the UK
8  Celebrated on 31st October
9  Invaded by the U.S. and UK in 2003
10  Usually staged at Christmas time
12  All working UK citizens must pay National...

## Down

1  A Spanish invasion of ships
2  The elected house of parliament
6  National healthcare provider
7  The currency in the UK is pound
11  The party that won the 1997 general election

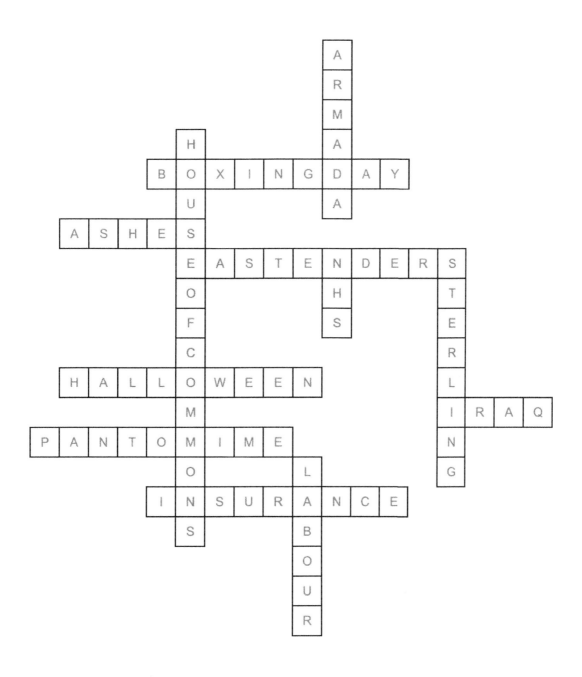

# Famous Faces

Name these famous faces from British sport, politics and culture

NAME

NAME

NAME

NAME

NAME

NAME

NAME

Clement Attlee

NAME

Andy Murray

NAME

William Beverage

NAME

Alfred Hitchcock

NAME

Margaret Thatcher

NAME

Tony Blair

# ONLINE COURSE

The online course designed to help you pass the official Home Office 'Life in The UK' test. Covering over 10,000 years of British history as well as life in Britain today. The course follows the 'Life in The United Kingdom Handbook: A Guide for New Residents' issued by the UK Government.

# TIMED PRACTICE TESTS

The life in the UK online course includes 100s of practice questions so you can practice under exam conditions. Each practice test includes 24 multiple choice questions which you will have 45 minutes to answer, this is exactly the same format as the real test. The practice questions will help you to consolidate your knowledge and make sure you are ready to sit the real test.

# Learn on the Go

It is up to you when and where you learn. Login from any device and jump straight back in where you left off. Most of our learners complete the Life in The UK Course in less than 30 days. You can monitor your progress with our built in progress bar so you can see how much of the course you have completed. You can take the mock tests at any time and can re-take them throughout the course to test what you have learned.

We are constantly updating the tests and content to make sure we cover the kind of questions you will be asked in the official test. When you enroll on the 100% online course you will have access to all of the future mock tests we create too.

# We Speak Your Language

You can translate the course content into any language with Google Translate integrated directly in the learning platform. Whether you speak Spanish, Chinese, Italian, Polish, French or German we've got you covered. Check out the language drop down at the top of the page...

# 50% OFF FOR READERS

Get 50% off the full online course (usually £29). Go to **liveintheuk.co.uk** and use the discount code below when you checkout.

**50BOOK**

Printed in Great Britain
by Amazon